REASON & VIOLENCE

ALSO BY R. D. LAING

The Divided Self
Self and Others
Reason and Violence
(with David Cooper)
Sanity, Madness and the Family, Vol. 1:
The Families of Schizophrenics
(with Aaron Esterson)
Interpersonal Perception: A Theory and a Method of Research
(with H. Phillipson and A. R. Lee)
The Politics of Experience
The Politics of the Family
Knots
The Facts of Life
Do You Love Me?
Conversations with Adam and Natasha
Sonnets
The Voice of Experience

ALSO BY D. G. COOPER

Psychiatry and Anti-Psychiartry
The Death of the Family

R. D. LAING

REASON &

D. G. COOPER

VIOLENCE

A DECADE OF SARTRE'S PHILOSOPHY 1950-1960

FOREWORD BY JEAN-PAUL SARTRE

PANTHEON BOOKS, NEW YORK

Library of Congress Cataloging in Publication Data

Laing, R. D. (Ronald David), 1927–
   Reason and violence.
   Includes Index.
   1. Sartre, Jean Paul, 1905–   . I. Cooper, David Graham. II. Title.
B2430.S34L3 1983   194   83-2470   ISBN 0-394-71582-9 (pbk.)

Manufactured in the United States of America

First Pantheon Paperback Edition

CONTENTS

I have read with great attention the book that you were kind enough to send me. It is, I am happy to say, a very clear, very faithful account of my thought. In addition to your perfect understanding of my *La Critique de la Raison Dialectique*, what attracted me in this and your earlier works was your constant concern to find an 'existential' approach to the mentally sick. Like you, I believe that one cannot understand psychological disturbances *from the outside*, on the basis of a positivistic determinism, or reconstruct them with a combination of concepts that remain outside the illness as lived and experienced. I also believe that one cannot study, let alone cure, a neurosis without a fundamental respect for the person of the patient, without a constant effort to grasp the basic situation and to relive it, without an attempt to rediscover the response of the person to that situation, and—like you, I think—I regard mental illness as the 'way out' that the free organism, in its total unity, invents in order to be able to live through an intolerable situation. For this reason, I place the highest value on your researches, in particular on the study that you are making of the family as a group and as a series—and I am convinced that your efforts will bring closer the day when psychiatry will, at last, become a truly *human* psychiatry.

9 November 1963

JEAN-PAUL SARTRE
(translated into English
by A. M. Sheridan Smith)

6

J'ai lu attentivement l'ouvrage que vous avez bien voulu me confier et j'ai eu le grand plaisir d'y trouver un exposé très clair et très fidèle de ma pensée. Plus encore que votre parfaite intelligence de *La Critique de la Raison Dialectique*, ce qui me séduit en ce livre comme dans vos œuvres antérieures, c'est votre souci constant de réaliser une approche 'existentielle' des malades mentaux. Je pense comme vous qu'on ne peut comprendre les troubles psychiques *du dehors*, à partir du déterminisme positiviste ni les reconstruire par une combinaison de concepts qui restent extérieurs à la maladie vécue. Je crois aussi qu'on ne peut étudier ni guérir une névrose sans un respect originel de la personne du patient, sans un effort constant pour saisir la situation de base et pour la revivre, sans une démarche pour retrouver la réponse de la personne à cette situation—et je tiens—comme vous, je crois—la maladie mentale comme l'issue que le libre organisme, dans son unité totale, invente pour pouvoir vivre une situation invivable. Par cette raison, j'attache le plus grand prix à vos recherches, en particulier à l'étude que vous tentez du milieu familial pris comme groupe et comme série—et je suis convaincu que vos efforts contribuent à nous rapprocher du temps où la psychiatrie sera, enfin, *humaine*.

Je vous remercie de la confiance que vous m'avez témoignée et je vous prie de croire à mon estime très attentive.

le 9 novembre 1963   JEAN-PAUL SARTRE

The three works expounded in this volume, *Saint Genet, Comédien et Martyr* (1952),[1] *Questions de Méthode* (1960),[2] and *Critique de la Raison Dialectique* (1960),[3] together make up a vast verbal edifice.

Condensation to about one-tenth of the scale of the original clearly creates its own difficulties. We have chosen the more rigorous and, to some, perhaps the more arid path of following the main lines of Sartre's thought, without giving much space to his own, often lengthy, illustrations.

Marx is credited with the remark that he had no time to write short books. This can be said to be a long short book—long to write, no doubt long to read. We are dealing at every point with key ideas. Theoretical decisions at this level have consequences in a multitude of practical affairs. We are concerned with decisive issues over man's understanding of himself. Here we have a most ambitious theoretical venture—no less than a *totalization*, as Sartre puts it, of the whole of existing socio-historical knowledge. Here is a systematic theory that aims to comprehend the whole range from individual phantasy, interpersonal relations, socio-technical systems, to inter-group relations. Sartre aims to be systematic, without pretending to present a closed and finished system; this totalization in progress perpetually abdicates any pretensions or intentions to finished totality.

In what follows we shall make brief comments, first, on certain of Sartre's pivotal terms and concepts; second, on the relation of the works here under notice to linguistic philosophy, sociology, psycho-analysis, and Marxism.

[1,2,3] Paris: Librairie Gallimard. English translations: [1] *Saint Genet*, New York: Knopf; London: W. H. Allen, 1963; [2] *Search for a Method*, New York: Braziller, 1963; *The Problem of Method*, London: Methuen, 1964.

Sartre tends to employ his terms, rather than to define them. This is consistent with his dialectical strategy, because, at each level of concreteness, Sartre's terms take on new significations, and subsume the old ones in larger syntheses.

The dialectic for Sartre is a method both for working up to the experience of the concrete, and for developing a conceptual scheme adequate to such experience. But this experiential-conceptual strategy is not all. If knowing is a necessary interplay between percept and concept, each feeding the other, there is still the question of that which is perceived and conceived.

In Sartre's view, there is one realm of being where dialectical principles are constitutive of the nature of the known itself. This is the realm of human history. As for the processes of the non-human world, the realm of natural science, the dialectic can furnish regulative but not constitutive principles. Thus, in the realm of the human, Sartre uses dialectic to characterize both the relation between the knower and the known, and the nature of the known. Presumably alluding to Durkheim, he remarks that social facts are things to the extent that things are social facts.

We recall that Kant's table of categories consists of four groups of three. The third in each group is arrived at by a synthesis of the first and second. Kant's concept of synthesis is at least germinally dialectical in the Hegel-Marx-Sartre sense. Kant's first group is particularly pertinent to Sartre's present work. The synthesis of plurality and unity is a totality—a multiplicity-in-unity or a unified multiplicity. But, for Sartre, there are no final totalities in history. There are only totalizations-detotalizations-retotalizations. Sartre uses the term totalization both for the act of totalizing the field of the given, and for the field that is totalized. These objects or subjects totalized or totalizing, multiplicities synthetically unified by the others, or by the individuals who themselves comprise them, provide the key to the understanding of history.

A totalization, somehow dissociated from the act that constitutes it, established as a finished entity once and for all, would be a totality. But Hegel and Marx have shown that the very condition of change, of history, is that each totalization is subject to detotalization.

In the *Phenomenology of Mind*, Hegel sought to show that many facets of reality can be unified into a consistent view of the world, in terms of which particular events, experiences, actions, find their place and can be construed accordingly. However, another synthesis, equally self-consistent, equally systematic, and seemingly all-embracing, can be found, in the light of which the same happenings or the same situation can be construed in ways that completely contradict the former. Each particular perspective, each particular point of view, is the centre of a world, but not the centre of another world. Each point of view is an absolute, and at the same time absolutely relative: collisions between points of view occasion endless instability; collusions are efforts at some measure of stabilization.

Hegel's method of investigating the endless relentless cancellation of one viewpoint by another, was his dialectic. Each point of view first seems the whole truth. Then from another point of view the first synthesis of the situation, the first *totalization*, as Sartre puts it, turns out to be relative, and, we suspect, even perhaps completely false, so plausible may the second point of view come to appear. But then one finds that there is a third, fourth, fifth . . . n + 1 perspective, each, while we are absorbed in it, more convincing, more systematic in its elaboration of a synthesis, than the others, and no point of view is more plausible to the sceptic than scepticism of all points of view, including his own. No totalization *can* be a totality, embodying final truth. None need, by the same token, be totally false. Each is relative, and, as relative, each can have relative validity. One finds oneself making a synthesis in turn of all other syntheses that one can conceive of. One may pride oneself that one's own synthesis contains the overall truth—until such hubris is humbled before the realization that this in turn cannot but be devoured in another synthesis, detotalized in another's totalization, and so on, *ad infinitum*.

By the *act* of perceiving a *number* (of people) as *one*, a group begins to be formed. This act of rudimentary group-synthesis brackets, as it were, a number of human beings together. I bracket you and him together—I both perceive you and him, and I think of you and him together as You or Them. 'You' or 'Them' is now a social entity, a social gestalt, that I have *constituted* as such for me by making one social whole out of two singular individuals. One and one make one.

But this new total, this fusion of unity and plurality, is not an easy operation to describe. Sartre explores the nature of these human *totalizations* phenomenologically: and this now is the same as to say dialectically. He explores non-analogically. A totalization is an act; it changes the agent, the acted-upon, and their relation. And this dialectic can *only* be studied dialectically. Sartre contends that the categories of what he calls analytic and positive reason fail us here, and that it is only in and through a form of reason adequate to the reality before us that we *can* think it, to use 'think' transitively. That is, to think is a type of praxis, the object thought a type of deed. He does not explicitly refer to Vico in this work, but it seems that, for both, *verum factum*.

To think non-dialectically upon any aspect of the range of human history, in Sartre's view, is necessarily to falsify our percepts to fit our concepts, to distort our concrete experience by reifications, extrapolations, abstractions, persistently false analogies, and other operations, to knead it to a form with which analytic-positive reason can cope. We try to constitute human reality into a form that does violence to its own nature.

Sartre regards analytic reason as a reflection of the way European society was structured for a time. That time has passed but its reflection persists, and is blending now into contemporary forms. But no possible transformation of analytic-positive reason (and it can excel in 'sophistication') can give us understanding of our present forms of alienation, of which it is itself an exemplar. It has no way whereby it can conceive of the social meaning of nothing and negation, and no means of thinking the changing movement of history. It may then make a virtue of its own impotence; or lapse into a totalistic determinist historicism, or its antipode, a hyperempiricism.

A key concept is Hegel's *aufheben*. Sartre's term is *dépasser*. A totalization holds the field. It is challenged by another totalization. The first totalization loses its absolute validity, conserves a relative validity, and becomes absorbed into the second, if the second is sufficiently encompassing. Thus it is negated as an absolute, conserved as a relative, and subsumed in the later synthesis. And this synthesis will in turn be subsumed in another, and this in another, and so on.

A point of view, a synthesis, a totalization, in being *depassed* in this threefold way, becomes a historical moment.

We have used a variety of terms for the rich inflections of the principal threefold connotations of *aufheben* and *dépasser*. The French word is enviably ordinary and urbane. It can be used for one car passing another and leaving it behind. We have occasionally coined an English translation of one of the forms of this word, viz. *indepassable*, but for the most part we have used such terms as to negate, to annul, to conserve, to go beyond, to transcend.

Sartre asks what are the different ways in which totalizations are constituted—the different ways, for instance, that I or you or him or we, you or them, group ourselves together or against one another. The totalization will be different in terms of whether I and you constitute ourselves as *we*, or whether I constitute you and him as *them*, or whether it is he who constitutes me and you as them-for-him, when you and I may not wish to constitute ourselves as *we*, etc. What are the properties of certain key totalizations?

There are totalizations of varying transience and permanence, and with varying degrees and kinds of structure and process, and organization and institutionalization.

All totalizations are social realities of some kind or other, and there are many subdivisions of them. What sort of beings are they? What is their ontological status? Are they objective realities? Are they subjective realities? Are they facts or figments—and in what sense? For instance, what is the being of the

'Jews' for a Nazi, or an Arab for a Jew, or the 'Niggers' for a White lyncher, or a 'Red' for a rabid anti-Communist, or a 'red fascist' for a Reichian cultist?

We 'constitute' ourselves and others into social collectivities by acts of totalization. Sartre's view is that such collectivities are real and actual. They exist in so far as we (whoever we are) have constituted them (whoever they are, they may be us)— and they exist in so far as, and only in so far as, we continue to constitute them—or, as Sartre sometimes puts it, in so far as we *invent* them. He traces out different ways of seeking permanence for various totalizations, different attempts to guarantee against detotalizations that threaten from different sources, some necessary *a priori*, some contingent.

In the last and crucial resort, even the most apparently permanent institutionally preserved human group is ultimately maintained by the concerted invention of its being. What techniques are required to keep groups as groups? It seems that there is a constant struggle to constitute and preserve, and to attack and destroy, these peculiar constituted 'beings', if not always the singular individuals who comprise them. It may be difficult to destroy a group 'being' without destroying the individuals who make it up. Here is another crucial question. What is the relation(s) of the group 'being' to the human beings who comprise it?

Efforts to articulate this often short-circuit the issue by analogical thinking—the group as a Leviathan, as a supra-individual, as a whole to parts, as an organism, as a mechanism. No positive generalized answer can be given, but Sartre undertakes a detailed analysis in the case of each type of totalization in question. Since Sartre's effort is to achieve the concrete, perceptually and conceptually, in following his spiral dialectic movement of synthesis upon synthesis, we pass many social theorists going hard in the opposite direction.

However, in the light of Sartre's own totalization of the perceptions and conceptions of collectivities, one can locate the type and degree of abstraction and reification employed in various theories, wittingly or unwittingly, and hence the violence done perceptually and conceptually to the human reality in its concrete full being.

One can develop theories that are outgrowths from different levels of abstraction and extrapolation of the full concreteness of the human. One can have a theory of mind unrelated to the body, a theory of behaviour unrelated to experience, a theory of the individual unrelated to society, a theory of society unrelated to the individual, a theory of persons or society unrelated to the material world.

Sartre sees the various theories of sociology, anthropology, and psycho-analysis as more or less partial realizations of some moment or moments in the dialectic. Since they are not grasped by dialectical reason they are blown up into total theories, and inevitably run into contradictions which their authors try to deal with by *ad hoc* hypotheses, or simply ignore.

Thus a whole theory of society will be elaborated starting from the conflict between classes, without any adequate grasp of the classes themselves being constituted by a prior dialectic beginning with praxis.

Yet again, a total pluralism of individual agents will be posited without realizing that the concrete individual is always riddled by the particular metamorphoses he undergoes in being a member of particular groups. There is no such human being as a non-grouped individual. The individual's actions always and everywhere occur within the context of concerted group experiences, rights-obligations, command-obedience structures, and so on, and thus the scheme for the intelligibility of his actions requires to have many more dialectic spirals than that required for the conception of an imaginary single individual in an unmediated person-person, or person-to-world, relationship.

The reader taking up Sartre's *Critique of Dialectical Reason* may well have uncomfortable and perhaps irritated feelings of being mystified by this epic of philosophical, sociological, and psychological demystification. He looks around for signposts or land-marks and finds none, or rather he finds signposts that deceive him, leading him into blind alleys of speculation in which he rapidly loses sight of the busy main street of discourse. There are some references to a few writers, notably to Hegel and Marx, but he soon discovers that even these are not straightforward indications of continuity or of discontinuity in a tradition. The reader struggles to identify himself with this thought, as a pre-requisite to attaining a critical distance. But this thought is perpetually altering its perspective: one moment it studies its object, the next moment it reflexively thinks itself, inventing itself as it examines itself. Unless he begins to live this totalizing venture himself, the reader may despair. In any case he is likely to experience a sort of vertigo.

If, despite the guidance and orientation provided in *Questions of Method*, the reader has this difficulty in orientating himself and what he reads in relation to the tradition of other philosophers, neither is it easy to rely on Sartre's earlier writings for his bearings. To use one of Sartre's favourite expressions, these works are now *dépassé*. Being-for-itself and being-in-itself, the fundamental categories of *Being and Nothingness*, are absorbed into praxis and process. In fact, the *pour soi* is mentioned only once, almost dis-missively, in a footnote in the *Critique*. This may seem disconcerting but is not a rejection by Sartre of his philosophical past. The key positions of the earlier work are conserved in the later, but con-served through a dialectical transformation as one moment in the later synthesis.

Fortunately, *Saint Genet*, in so far as it states a philosophical position, may be regarded as transitional from the earlier phil-osophy to the later. In this work we still find the categories of *Being and Nothingness*: good and bad faith, the dialectic of freedom, the three ontological dimensions of the body. (These no longer appear in the *Critique*.) But, together with biographical analysis in terms of these categories, we discover an increasingly explicit and systematic concern with the relation between the individual person and the groups, institutions, and class to which he belongs. We comprehend Genet's abandonment by his mother and the adoptive peasant family in the Morvan as the mode of his insertion into social and historical reality. The phenomenology of institutional serialization is explored in detail (e.g. Genet's experience of himself as a number in the register of the *Assistance Publique*). The relations between the 'societies' of producers and consumers, the fusion and development of a group based on reciprocal loyalty and its progressive institutionalization by the 'female' criminals, as opposed to the tough 'males', are all worked out as ways the person is himself metamorphosed through his participation in different forms of sociality. All Genet's relations with the Other, as Sartre describes them, are *group relations*. Genet is another to the other and also 'third' to himself and to the other. Throughout this study the negative relation of existential analysis both to psycho-analysis and to Marxist explanation is exemplified concretely but not with full explicitness and rigour, for this clearly required a special work.

Such wide-ranging activity on the part of a philosopher must seem to lack any point of contact with the British philosophical scene, particularly if one refers to that dominant tradition which runs from Russell and G. E. Moore, through Wittgenstein of the early and late phases, to the organized professional philosophers of linguistic analysis. This is no place to delineate the disjunction between the more or less constant core of assumptions of linguistic analysis and the views of Sartre, but we may be permitted some reflections on opposed views of language.

To point out the ambiguities of language is one thing: the wish to eliminate them is another. There may be good reasons why a piece of colloquial language or a philosophical proposition is ambiguous. The ambiguity may be the result of a mystified and mystifying attitude of mind, but, on the other hand, it may very appropriately mirror an ambiguous fact.

It could even be that the human reality in which we live is ambiguous in its essence, and that this is reality for philosophers too. Sartre seeks to demonstrate this, not only in the works we consider here, but in all his philosophical works, his novels, and his theatre.

Ambiguous facts are evident when we view a person from various perspectives with various conceptual frameworks. Psychologically the statement 'I hate you!' may mean what it seems to say, but at the same time, when understood within the total context of a relationship, it may equally mean 'I love you'. It does not help to say that the meaning (signification) of the signs 'I hate you!' on this page is really 'I love you!' Moreover, the words uttered may express simultaneous feelings of love and hatred. Socially and politically the realization which leads me to exclaim 'I am bourgeois' may signify my further imprisonment of myself in a class role which is lived as part of my essence or nature, but simultaneously it may signify a liberation by unveiling fresh possibilities of changing this aspect of what I am by political acts which help to change the class structure of society. Ontologically I am a being related to myself in an ambiguous way. There is a sense in which my identity must be recognized: there is also a sense that I am not what I am. As Sartre has put it, following Heidegger, I am a being such that my being is in question to itself. This ontological ambiguity of human reality is the very pivot of *Being and Nothingness*, and this notion still pervades the later synthesis of the *Critique*, though not expressed in these terms.

Language has developed within limits imposed by the degree of self-consciousness which man has attained. The analytic-instrumental approach to the world and to oneself entails a language which expresses the results of the analytic process, but the language then expresses an analytically *reduced* reality. Existing languages are all imperfectly adapted to the expression of some aspects of reality. But by what law do we subjugate ourselves and our philosophical vision to such languages or to logically perfected versions of them in which each 'atomic proposition' 'reflects' each 'atomic fact'? Such atomization of the world and of language is the product of a human praxis, a project of atomization, but, as we shall see, the notion of project entails the notion of a person as a synthetic unity. One is forced by the reality one is into a reflective meta-position in relation to such views.

When we have to deal with ambiguous facts in language that tries to be non-ambiguous, we inevitably arrive at a new level of ambiguity. Sartre's writing is full of ambiguities but these are ambiguities which he exploits in the service of communication. Communication is a precise word here since Sartre is not centrally concerned with *communion*. Sartre recognizes that the prose writer, at his moment of success, having arrived at meanings that outstrip the language, meanings that are in a sense secreted between the lines of his pages, cannot do more than reveal what he cannot say. All great prose is a special kind of failure. Yet the writer must play this game with despair if he is to honour his commitment to write philosophy which is not trivial.

The disjunction between everyday language and metaphysical language is more apparent than real. A child experiences himself, sometimes in a stupefying moment of revelation, as existing[1] a certain identity. He is himself and no other. He is an utterly separate, utterly contingent fact in the universe—but his destiny is in his hands and nowhere else. He then re-unites himself with the world. He returns to his family, and, more likely than not, he soon loses his self in the engulfing morass of alienating, serializing, massifying forces. In all probability he will never attempt to recapture, define, and express his experience in 'philosophical language', but if he does decide to write what language is he to use? His was not an everyday experience, but he takes everyday words and develops special meanings by placing them in certain ways in certain contexts. He may or may not, in addition, neologize from classical roots. He becomes aware of and controls and exploits the dialectical interaction between terms or issues and their linguistic context (their relation to other terms and other issues). Everyday language will not be adequate to express the significance of the childhood experience, nor perhaps of all the

[1] To use this verb, as Sartre does, transitively.

other germinal realizations from which philosophical totalizations develop. But language must be pressed into service even if
this involves turning language against itself, exploiting its
deficiencies, its vagueness, and its contradictions.

One has, in fact, through considerations of the 'naturalness' of
philosophizing, to question very basically the view that metaphysical language is different from or more prone to nonsense than
everyday language. The nonsense, in so far as it exists, is a measure
of the discrepancy between language and experience in so far as
experience perpetually outstrips the possibilities of linguistic
expression. We have to refer a person's utterances to the concrete
totality of his life if he has already lived it or to our totalization of
his totalization-in-process if he is still alive.

In the first year of life, experience, or rather our limited
inferences about it from our adult objectifying perspective, is
given no verbal expression. Phantastic worlds of primitive greed,
envy, cannibalistic destruction of parts of the Other's body and of
whole other persons precede the first distinguishable words. These
phantasies persist through all subsequent experiential totalizations,
conserved in their primitive violence through all the stages of
self-depassment of the self. The pre-verbal experience of the first
year of life forms a pre-reflective continuum with the paralinguistic
experience of the older child and adult.[1] Here we must limit
ourselves simply to indicating the problem of transforming into
language experiences which occur outside it.

My experience simultaneously seeks and flinches from its verbal
expression. My words become other-for-the-other. Language
is objectification, it is the occasion of the Other's appropriation
of my subjective reality. Sartre refers more than once in
his earlier work to the paranoid delusion that one's thoughts
are being 'stolen' by the other. This madness, however, is a confused expression of the ontological truth of language, which is
that its structure is always that of being-for-the-other. There is

[1] Laing, R. D., *Self and Others*, London: Tavistock Publications, 1961, second edition
1969; New York: Pantheon Books, 1969.

no private, interior language which does not have this structure. The inaudible utterances of my talking to myself reflect the way I am a quasi-other to myself.

There is no language-in-itself, distinct from the philosopher's objectification of himself for the other, in relation to which one can adopt the critical perspective of much of linguistic analysis. One can be sure that criticism in a similar vein will be made of the *Critique*, but those who take the trouble and have the capacity to re-examine basically their conceptions of rationality will find in this work a delineation of types of rationality and their limits and relation which must mark a new point of departure for philosophy as well as constituting the basis of a structural and historical anthropology which is its explicit aim.[1]

The three works we examine in this volume, apart from their presentation of a major philosophical totalization, address workers in specific disciplines. In particular they challenge sociologists and psycho-analysts.

Sartre refers explicitly to only a limited range of American social scientific thinking, which he refers to rather generically as 'American sociology'. He is critical of Kurt Lewin's method of looking at a group from outside it as 'fetishism of totalities'. He also attacks Kardiner's 'basic personality structure' produced in any given society by the 'primary institutions' of child-rearing that are specific to this culture. Kardiner's thinking is essentialistic and mechanistic. It is essentialistic in so far as a certain 'human nature' is ordained for each society; this nature by implication is indepassable, although it may change by an externally imposed acculturation process. It is mechanistic in so far as hyperorganismal qualities are reified and a sort of intentionality is attributed to them: 'Primary institutions were responsible for the basic personality structure which, in turn, was responsible for the secondary institutions.'[2] Such criticism, though necessary, does

[1] See Cooper, D. G., *Psychiatry and Anti-Psychiatry*, London: Tavistock Publications, 1967. The introduction deals with this question.

[2] Kardiner, A., 'Basic Personality Structure', p. 553 in *Psychological Theory*, edited by Melvin H. Marx, New York: Macmillan, 1951.

less than justice to Kardiner's work which, however tendentious its solutions, at least clearly outlines the problems posed by work such as Ruth Benedict's, in which the relations between institutions in a society are discussed analogically in terms of one-person psychopathology. Sartre does not deal adequately with later work in group dynamics that is indebted to Lewin, nor with the work of Talcott Parsons, Bales, Shils, and others. There is no indication by Sartre of awareness of the extent to which some of his fundamental criticisms have been anticipated by American sociologists themselves, for example, by Znaniecki in his account of the contradiction in sociology[1] between the viewpoint of 'social structure' and that of 'social change', as a result of which analysis proceeds from two isolated perspectives and the results are then simply added together.

Sartre, however, is also critical of so-called Marxist critiques of American sociology that make global judgements to the effect that most of this sociology provides ideological tools for the ruling class by which it can help to support itself. The criticism may be true in specific ways in specific cases, but this sociology has achieved a great deal of concrete success, and its methodological advances must be conserved in future social thinking. However, it lacks a philosophical orientation and its own internal crisis points to this lack. In a very real sense American sociology is on the brink of a totalizing vision which Marxism, when it overcomes its tendency to betray itself into mechanistic anti-dialectic idealism, should provide.

Psycho-analysis, like sociology, is an 'auxiliary discipline' which must find its place within the totalizing scheme. Like sociology, it provides vital mediations which have been lacking from conventional and conventionalized Marxist analyses. We shall not anticipate here Sartre's argument that psycho-analysis (apart from the shaky, speculative system-building enterprises of a few indifferent thinkers among psycho-analysts) does not

[1] Znaniecki, F., 'Basic Problems of Contemporary Sociology', *American Sociological Review*, Vol. 19, Oct. 1954.

conflict with a Marxist philosophical framework, since it has no theoretical basis but is simply a technique, an extremely good one, for investigating a vital sector of human reality. We shall, however, attempt to understand what Sartre understands by psycho-analysis.

Psycho-analysis for Sartre is above all an illumination of the present acts and experience of a person in terms of the way he has lived his family relationships. If a certain type of psycho-analytical thinking would reduce the complex realities of behaviour and experience to such 'pseudo-irreducibles' as an indepassable constitutional datum, an innate proportion of, say, life and death instinct, then existential criticism must set it on the correct course and help it to discover the intelligible choice of self, the fundamental project of becoming a certain sort of personal being. If we see personal life in Sartre's terms as 'constituted-constituting', as *a synthetic unity of what we make of what we are made of*, of moulding ourselves out of how we have been moulded, we must conclude that psycho-analytic theory in its weaker aspects ignores the active constituting, making, moulding moment of personal unity, thereby reducing the person to a resultant of instinctual vector-abstractions which leave no place for intentionality in each life.

This criticism needs authoritative and detailed statement, but Sartre, both in the present works and in the section entitled 'Existential Psycho-analysis' in *Being and Nothingness*, limits his dealings with psycho-analysis to a number of Freud's original metapsychological positions. He does not explicitly examine anything like the whole range of psycho-analytic writing in relation to his thesis.

This self-imposed limitation becomes particularly evident in *Saint Genet*. The incorporation of unconscious phantasy as a mode of experience would have added a further dimension of concrete richness to the analysis of the working-out of Genet's project, namely, to achieve personal identity and autonomy by choosing to be what the others would have him be. In *Notre-*

Dame des Fleurs, for instance, Genet's character Divine lists an 'inventory' of objects which are of personal significance to him. His 'phantasy' operation here is to project bits of himself, 'good' and 'bad' (ridiculous) aspects of his personality, into the inanimate objects (projective identification), to form them into a more or less unified series, the inventory, and then to re-interiorize the integrated result as a way of integrating himself. This transaction occurs in Divine's experience, and Genet's Divine is quite closely autobiographical. In writing of Divine, Genet exteriorizes and then re-interiorizes major aspects of himself in a similar self-integrative project on another level. This is a concrete amplification of what Sartre has referred to on an ontological level of discourse as a project of *récupération*. To see this as praxis on the part of Divine–Genet does not involve one in the false meta-phenomenological position of resorting to an indepassable biological constitution which vitiates much psycho-analytic writing.

The difference between Sartre's position and that of many psycho-analysts is seen most clearly in relation to the question of the limits of psycho-analysis. At a certain point in the process of explanation, many psycho-analysts find it necessary to switch perspective from that in which the observer makes his observations from the heart of a relationship, an interactional situation of reciprocal influence and change, to that in which the analyst attempts to make judgements about the analysand (a person) from a position of complete exteriority in relation to a biological entity. The person disappears. Sartre, on the other hand, traces the life of the person to its own ultimate issues, which are to be found only within personal life itself. This ultimate 'original project', or original choice of self, provides the intelligible basis of all the acts and experiences of the person. The reductive biologism prevalent in psycho-analytic thinking explains all, and it explains nothing. It explains all in the sense that, within the circumscribed conceptual framework of a psycho-organismal dualism (however 'holistically' sophisticated its expression),

ultimately perfected biochemical and neuro-physiological techniques, and carefully delineated instinctive units of behaviour,
will account 'correlatively' for every possible 'psychic drive' that
can be thought up. It explains nothing in so far as the person with
whom the psycho-analyst had supposed himself to be concerned
has evaporated from the field of discourse and we find ourselves
talking about something else, indeed about no one. It is only
through the discovery of a freedom, a choice of self functioning
in the face of all determinations, conditioning, fatedness, that we
can attain the comprehension of a person in his full reality.

The original project, always a relation of self to being, cannot
be expressed in physicalistic metaphor and biological analogy
without fatal confusion and ambiguity. Unfortunately even the
best psycho-analytic papers are written in these terms or fall back
into them. Indeed, it is often unclear when a psycho-analytic
writer supposes that he is being metaphorical or analogizing or
attempting an explanation. Too often the latter appears to be the
case, and the work becomes stultified with fetishized pseudo-
irreducibles.

There *is* plenty of room for a phenomenological examination
of 'unconscious phantasy', in so far as the latter is conceived in its
reality as experience and not as a series of mechanisms to be
imposed upon a subject objectified in the psycho-analytic
situation. One might, on this point, propose a marriage between
existential analysis and the structuralism of Jacques Lacan, who
so expertly articulates the 'language' of the unconscious. Petty
disputation regarding 'history' or 'History' should not delay the
ceremony.

Sartre affirms and strongly supports by impressive argument the
view that Marxism is the only possible philosophy for our age, and
then proceeds to examine fundamental epistemological positions
of Marxism and also specific types of concrete 'analysis of the
situation' made by Marxist or would-be Marxist writers. In this
he achieves what is both a radical critique and a radical confirmation
of Marxism. He shows how Marxism has undergone certain

deformations into mechanistic and idealistic thinking and how it has suffered a methodological sclerosis. But this is far from revisionism—revisionism, as he puts it, is reversion to pre-Marxism and therefore untenable. His desire is rather a project to restore to Marxism its original vital impulse. Conservative bureaucracy in the Stalin era ruined and finally paralysed this impulse, and even today in post-Stalinist socialist societies Marxism appears rarely to be allowed to come alive, to be lived in its pristine reality as 'disillusionment'.

The Marxists' comparative neglect of Sartre is remarkable, but perhaps it is not so surprising. In the same year in which the *Critique* was published a work entitled *Fundamentals of Marxism-Leninism* was published in Moscow under the editorship of the 'old Bolshevik' O. Kuusinen. In this work one finds, in certain sections, all the old Stalinist denunciatory clichés, about existentialism for instance, with no evidence that the authors have read existential philosophy, and certainly no evidence that they have worked at existential texts. Not many Marxist writers seem capable of giving an authoritative critical appraisal of the *Critique*.

Whatever inhibitions present-day 'orthodox' Marxists may have about reading or publicly debating Sartre's work, it is probable that Marxist thought will only continue its development when Marxists undertake a radical re-examination of their basic philosophical positions on the lines indicated by Sartre. This is necessary, since dialectical thought by its very definition not only must grasp its object but must reflexively grasp itself.

The scope of the works we consider here is immense. *Saint Genet* is a mature embodiment and application of Sartre's principles of existential biography. In so far as the method is valid it would provide a prototype for subsequent biographical statements for some time to come, including 'clinical' biography. It is perhaps the most radical attempt by one man to understand the life of another living man in its most basic terms recorded in literature.

Then, in the *Critique*, Sartre attempts to establish the dialectical bases of a structural anthropology. This work is critical in so far as, by an approach which is itself dialectical, it seeks to demarcate the limits and validity of dialectical reason, to determine affinities and oppositions of dialectical and analytical reason. In this first volume of the *Critique* we are presented with a theory of different ways in which totalizations are initially constituted and perpetuated. In the second volume Sartre promises to examine the possibility of a totalization of totalizations, that is to say, History itself.

If this project succeeds, Sartre will be not the philosopher of the age, for he has explicitly abdicated the role of protagonist of a philosophical system, but he will be the prime mover of one of the greatest syncretic revolutions in human thought. So one waits.

Although *Saint Genet*, as we have said, is transitional to *Questions of Method* and the *Critique*, and although Sartre has said that the *Questions* ought logically to follow the *Critique*, we have chosen to introduce the reader to the two large works through *Questions of Method*, since this represents a less formidable transition from prevalent categories of thought to the bold and systematic re-thinking in the works that follow it.

I. QUESTIONS OF METHOD

I. QUESTIONS OF METHOD

1. MARXISM AND EXISTENTIALISM

Philosophy does not exist. It is nothing but an hypostatized abstraction. There are only philosophies—or rather only one philosophy at a time which is alive. One philosophy gives expression to the general movement of society, and in so far as it is alive it serves as a cultural milieu for the men of that time. It presents itself simultaneously through very different aspects which it itself unifies. It is first of all a certain way that the ascendant class becomes conscious of itself. In the earliest phase of capitalism the bourgeoisie of merchants, jurists, and bankers glimpsed something of itself in Cartesianism, while a century later, in the primitive phase of industrialization, the bourgeoisie of manufacturers, engineers, and scientists obscurely discovered itself in the Kantian image of universal man.

But, in order to be truly philosophical, this mirror must present itself as the totalization of all contemporary knowledge. It must systematically develop itself in terms of certain directive schemata which translate into the realm of philosophical discourse the attitudes and techniques of the rising class, and in so doing it must unify all specific branches of knowledge. When the details have been challenged and destroyed the schemata remain, but they require facts to hold them together, as it were, as much as facts require them. The philosophical object remains in the 'objective spirit' as a regulative idea indicating an infinite task. While it is still alive, however, it is never this inert, passively determined unity. Born of social movement, it is itself movement and bites into the future. This concrete totalization is at the same time the abstract project to pursue unification to its ultimate limits. All philosophy is practical, even that which appears to be most purely contemplative. A philosophy remains effective only as long as the praxis which produced it remains alive—the praxis which maintains it and which it in turn illuminates.

Epochs of philosophical creation in this sense are rare. Between the seventeenth and twentieth centuries Sartre recognizes only three such philosophical moments: first, that of Descartes and of Locke; second, that of Kant and of Hegel; and, third, that of Marx. These three philosophies each became in their turn the stuff (humus) of all particular thought and the horizon of the whole culture. One could not go beyond them, since the historical moment which they expressed had not yet passed. In our present historical situation an 'anti-Marxist' argument is nothing more than a pre-Marxist idea, the pretended depassing of Marxism is at the worst only a return to pre-Marxism or at the best a re-discovery of an idea already contained in the supposedly depassed philosophy. As for 'revisionism', it is either a truism or an absurdity. One cannot re-adapt a living philosophy because it re-adapts itself through innumerable particular researches, because it is one with the movement of society. Now, if the movement of philosophy ceases, one of two things must be the case: either the philosophy is dead, in which case the rotten edifice must be rejected outright and not revised, or it is in a state of crisis. If the latter, the philosophical crisis is the particular expression of a social crisis, and its immobility is conditioned by the contradictions which tear asunder the society. Revision here can only be idealist mystification without the possibility of any real effect. It is the very movement of history, the conflict of men on all levels of human activity, which alone will free captive thought and allow it to reach its full development. In this precise sense Marxist philosophy is in a state of crisis.

Those who come after the great philosophical moments of

creation and who give a practical function to the theories, using them as tools for destruction and construction, are best not regarded as philosophers. They are nourished by the living thought of the great philosophers and are sustained by the movement of the masses of people. These *relative* beings Sartre calls *ideologists*. When he speaks of existentialism he understands it as an ideology, a parasitic system which exists on the margin of Knowing, which at first opposed itself to Knowing but which now attempts to integrate itself in it.

The most extensive philosophical totalization was made by Hegel. Sartre compares Kierkegaard with Hegel. Kierkegaard was assuredly not a philosopher and himself refused this title.

'For Hegel the Signifying (at a certain moment of history) is the movement of Spirit (which will constitute itself as signifying-signified and signified-signifying, that is to say as absolute-subject); the Signified is the living man and his objectivation; for Kierkegaard man is the Signifying, he produces the significations himself and no signification comes to him from the outside. . . .'[1]

Man is never the signified, not even signified by God. In attempting to place Kierkegaard in the setting of his epoch, Sartre says that Kierkegaard is right as opposed to Hegel, to the same extent as Hegel is right as opposed to Kierkegaard. Hegel is right in so far as, unlike Kierkegaard, he does not concern himself with fixed and impoverished paradoxes which refer finally to an empty subjectivity. He fixes in his concepts the truly concrete and the enriching mediation between Knowing and Being is always present. On the other hand, Kierkegaard is right in so far as pain, need, and suffering are brute human realities which cannot be depassed or changed by knowing alone. To be sure, his religious subjectivism can be regarded as an extreme idealism, but in relation to Hegel he makes progress to realism in so far as he insists on

[1] See *Questions*, p. 18.

the primacy of a certain reality and on its irreducibility to thought.

Certain psychologists and psychiatrists consider the evolution of our inner (*intime*) life as the result of *work* which we perform on ourselves. In this sense Kierkegaard's 'existence' is the work of our interior life, resistances overcome and ceaselessly renewed, temporary failures and precarious victories—this work being directly opposed to intellectual knowledge. Unlike Hegel, but thanks to him, Kierkegaard established the incommensurability of the Real and Knowing. This incommensurability can be the origin of a conservative irrationalism, but it is necessarily the death of absolute idealism. Ideas alone do not change men. But when, as at present in our society, there is a contradiction between productive forces and relations of production, the producer is estranged from his objectification in his product and his very labour appears to him as an alien force. It is necessary to live this contradiction in one's flesh and blood and bones, to live their conflicts with one's feelings. In short to work oneself or work through oneself (*se travailler*).

Marx, of course, addressed the same reproach to Hegel, although from a completely different point of view. For Marx, Hegel has confused objectification, the simple exteriorization of man in the universe, with alienation, which returns his exteriorization against man. Objectification permits man, ceaselessly producing his life, transforming himself as he changes nature, to contemplate himself in a world which he has created. But real history is based on actual alienation, not on a play of concepts, and no Hegelian sleight-of-hand can help man to escape it.

Marx stresses the priority of action (work and social praxis) to thought. Like Kierkegaard, he maintains that the human fact cannot be reduced to knowledge—it must be lived and produced. However, he does not confuse this with the empty subjectivity of a puritanical and mystified petit-bourgeois but he makes it the theme of a philosophical totalization. The concrete man in his struggle with things and other men is placed at the centre of his researches.

At one and the same time Marx is right as opposed to Hegel and to Kierkegaard. Like Hegel, he is concerned with the concrete man in his objective reality; like Kierkegaard he affirms the specificity of human existence. Under these conditions it seems that existentialism, as an idealist protest against idealism, has no further place and indeed it was eclipsed. In its fight against Marxism, bourgeois thought at first relied upon the post-Kantians, on Kant himself, and on Descartes. Only in the twentieth century, at a stage when for the first time bourgeois thought was reduced to the defensive, did Kierkegaard reappear, when pluralisms, ambiguities, and paradoxes were used against the Marxist dialectic. Between the two world wars a German existentialism appeared as a stealthy attempt to resuscitate the transcendent. Sartre writes that he is speaking here at least of Jaspers, and that the case of Heidegger is too complex to be examined (*exposé*) in this book. Jaspers has essentially done little more than comment on his master Kierkegaard. His originality consists solely in placing certain themes in relief and masking others. For example, the transcendent at first appears to be absent from his thought but in fact it haunts his thinking. We learn to sense it through our setbacks and failures of which it is supposed to be the profound meaning. This theme was less in relief in Kierkegaard, who lived in an age of revealed religion. Jaspers is silent over religious revelation and takes us via discontinuity, pluralism, and impotence, to a pure and formal subjectivity which discovers itself and its transcendence in the course of its failures. Success, as objectivation, allows the person to inscribe himself on things and thus obliges him to depass himself. Meditation on failure suits very well the partially dechristianized bourgeoisie, which regrets the faith it has lost because it has lost its trust in its rationalist and positivist ideology. Kierkegaard had already come to regard all victory as suspect because it turns man away from himself. Jaspers extracts from this position a subjectivistic pessimism which leads on to a theological optimism that does not dare announce itself as what it is. The transcendent for Jaspers remains veiled and is only apprehended by its absence. Pessimism is not depassed but one senses (*pressentir*) the reconciliation while remaining on the level of an insurmountable contradiction. This condemnation of the dialectic is directed not against Hegel but against Marx. Jaspers no longer refuses knowing, he refuses praxis. Kierkegaard refused to be a concept in the Hegelian system, but Jaspers refuses to be an individual in the Marxist's history. Kierkegaard progressed from Hegel in affirming the reality of the experienced, but Jaspers is historically regressive in fleeing from the real movement of praxis into abstract subjectivity, the end of which is to attain a certain inner (*intime*) quality, at once immanent and transcendent, which he calls existence. Philosophically this soft and underhand thought is a survival of no great interest, but there is another existentialism which has developed on the margin of Marxism and not against it and it is this existentialism which Sartre proclaims and with which we shall be concerned.

When he was a student Sartre read *Capital* and *The German Ideology* and he says he then understood both everything and nothing at all. To understand is to change oneself, to go beyond in the process of understanding, but at the university his reading of Marx did not change him. On the contrary that which changed him later was the *reality* of Marxism, the massive presence on his horizon of the working class which practised and lived Marxism. The universities lacked a Hegelian tradition, and it was permitted to study Marxism only so as to be able to 'refute' it. Sartre here makes intelligible his progress towards Marxism and then poses the question: 'Why then has existentialism preserved its autonomy? Why has it not been dissolved in Marxism?'

In a small volume entitled *Existentialism and Marxism*, Lukács, the Hungarian philosopher, believes he has replied to this question. He advances the thesis that the bourgeois intellectuals have been compelled to abandon idealism while completely preserving its results and foundations, because of the historical necessity in the bourgeois consciousness in the period of imperialism of having a 'third way' between idealism and materialism.

Sartre states that he will show what ravages this type of *a priori* conceptualization has caused in the heart of Marxism, but for the moment he observes that Lukács has taken no account of the principal fact of his, Sartre's, Marxism and existentialism, namely that he is convinced both that historical materialism provides the only valid interpretation of history *and at the same time* that existentialism remains the only concrete approach to reality. Sartre acknowledges the contradictions in this attitude but says that Lukács does not even suspect the fact. Many intellectuals live the tension of this double necessity which springs from a circumstance which Lukács knows only too well but about which he seems unable to say anything. After having liquidated all our bourgeois categories of thought and transformed all our ideas, Marxism abruptly leaves us in the lurch, unable to satisfy our need to comprehend the world from the particular situation in which we are placed. It can teach us nothing new because it is arrested.

In the early phase of the Soviet Union when it was solitary, encircled by capitalist states, and commencing its gigantic task of industrialization, ideology was subordinated to the needs of security and the construction of socialism in the Soviet Union, that is to say to unity. Paradoxically, the outcome of the drive for unity was that practice and theory were split apart in the transformation of practice into an empiricism without principles, and of theory into pure and rigid knowledge.

Sartre proceeds to consider examples of present-day Marxist thinking. The present-day Marxist deals not with living totalities, as did Marx, but with fixed entities—with what Sartre calls *general singularities*. He discusses one Marxist interpretation (an anti-Soviet one) of the Hungarian insurrection: according to this construction, hesitant and uncertain Soviet politics are conceptually fixed as the entity 'Soviet bureaucracy' and the reality of the Workers' Councils disappears into the abstract entity 'direct democracy'. The formal unities of these abstract and universal notions are then endowed with real powers. These thinkers are thus guilty of a fetishization of their own purely formal entities. We are left with a contradiction between two platonic ideas.

Living Marxism is heuristic: in relation to its concrete research its principles and its antecedent knowledge appear as *regulators*. Marx himself deals with living totalities (such as the petite bourgeoisie in the 18 Brumaire[1]), which define *themselves* in the course of his exposition. Unless one deals with living totalities, the importance which Marxists attach to the *analysis* of the situation becomes meaningless. Analysis of the situation does not suffice in itself, it is the first moment of a synthetic reconstruction —but it *is* necessary for the posterior reconstruction of the interplay of complex events. Today, however, analysis is reduced to a simple ceremony and it is no longer a matter of studying the facts in the general perspective of Marxism to enrich our knowledge and illuminate actions. The analysis consists in eliminating details, in forcing meaning into certain events, and in denaturing the facts so as to derive as their substance 'synthetic notions' which are immutable and fetishized. The open concepts of Marxism are now closed, they are no longer keys, interpretative schemata, but pose as knowledge already totalized. Instead of searching for the whole through the parts, and thus enriching the specificity of each part by seeing its polyvalent significations, which is the heuristic principle, we encounter the liquidation of particularity.

In American sociology we have real acquisitions but theoretical uncertainty. Psycho-analysis got off to a flying start, but has tended to become fixed and rigid with a great deal of detailed knowledge, but lacking a theoretical base. Marxism, on the other hand, has a theoretical base, it embraces all human activity, *but it no longer knows anything*, its concepts are *Diktats*. Its aim is no longer to acquire knowledge but to constitute itself *a priori* as absolute knowing. As against this double ignorance (sociology and psycho-analysis on the one hand and Marxism on the other) existentialism has been able to renew and maintain itself. Sartre

[1] The 18 Brumaire of Louis-Napoleon Bonaparte. The 18 Brumaire, in the revolutionary calendar, refers to Napoleon's *coup d'état* on 9 November 1799.

makes it clear that in referring to existentialism here he is referring to his own and no other kind of existentialism. Existentialism and Marxism have the same object. But Marxism has absorbed man into the idea while existentialism searches for man *everywhere where he is*, at work, in the street, in himself. Man is *not unknowable* but he is *unknown*. It is amazing that history in our age is made without reflective knowledge—as has always been the case. The very essence of Marxism, its power and richness, was that this should no longer be the case, but for the last twenty years Marxism has obscured history with its shadow. It has ceased to live *with* history and it has attempted through bureaucratic conservatism to reduce change to identity.

This sclerosis is not a normal aging process. Far from being exhausted, Marxism is young, almost in its infancy. It is commencing its development with great difficulty. It remains the indepassable philosophy of our time because the circumstances which gave rise to it are not depassed. Existentialism, like Marxism, approaches experience to discover concrete syntheses. These syntheses can only be conceived in the interior of a moving, dialectical totalization which is history, or—from the strictly cultural point of view which we are taking here—the world-of-becoming of philosophy. *Truth becomes.* It is and will be becoming. It is a totalization which ceaselessly totalizes itself. Particular facts signify nothing, are neither true nor false except in so far as they are related by the mediation of different partial totalities to the totalization-in-progress.

Sartre states his agreement with certain fundamental statements on Marxism by Garaudy[1] and Engels.[2] He takes the Marxist

[1] The statement to which Sartre refers is: 'Marxism to-day forms in fact the only system of coordinates which permits us to situate and define thought of any type, from political economy to physics, from history to ethics' (Garaudy: *L'Humanité*, 17 May 1955).

[2] '. . . men make their history themselves but in a given environment which conditions them, on the basis of real anterior conditions among which the economic conditons (however much influenced they may be by other, political and ideological conditions) are in the last analysis nothing less than the determining conditions which constitute throughout its length the conducting wire which leads us to understanding' (Engels quoted by Sartre, *Questions*, p. 30).

definition of materialism as 'the primacy of existence over consciousness'—which Lukács has used to distinguish Marxism from existentialism—and tells us that for existentialism, as even its name indicates, this primacy is the object of an affirmation of principle.

The only valid theory of knowledge today is one which is founded on that principle of microphysics which asserts that the experimenter is part of the experimental system. Only a theory so founded can eliminate all idealistic illusion and show us a real man in the midst of a real world, but this realism entails a reflexive point of departure: that is to say, the unveiling of a situation is achieved in and through the praxis which changes it. This does not mean that consciousness is placed at the source of action, but that we see it at the source as a necessary moment of the action itself.

Theory of knowledge, however, remains the weak point of Marxism. When Marx writes that 'the materialist conception of the world simply signifies the conception of nature as it is, without any foreign addition', he places himself in a position of pure exteriority from which he contemplates nature 'as it is', as a pure objective absolute. Having thus eliminated all subjectivity and having become part of a pure objective truth he walks about in a world of objects which is inhabited by men-objects. Lenin, on the other hand, writes that consciousness 'is only the reflection of being, in the best of cases an approximately exact reflection'. It seems thus that in Marxist epistemology there is a constituting consciousness which affirms *a priori* the rationality of the world (thereby falling into idealism) and which determines the constituted consciousness of each particular man as simple reflection (thereby ending in a sceptical idealism). Both these conceptions break the real relation between man and history. In the first knowledge is pure theory, non-situated observation, while in the second it is simple passivity. The conceptions cannot be assimilated to each other by a 'dialectical theory of reflection' for they are in essence anti-dialectical and 'pre-Marxist'. One can lapse into idealism not only by dissolving reality into subjectivity but also by denying real subjectivity in the name of objectivity. The truth is that subjectivity is neither all nor nothing: it is a moment of the objective process (that of the interiorization of exteriority) and this moment perpetually eliminates itself and is perpetually re-born.

II. THE PROBLEM OF MEDIATIONS AND AUXILIARY DISCIPLINES

Sartre commences the second part of *Questions of Method* with this question: If we accept the primacy of existence over consciousness and if we accept [as Sartre does] the more precise definition of materialism which Marx gives in *Capital*, i.e. 'The mode of production of material life in general dominates the development of social, political, and intellectual life'—why then are we not quite simply Marxists?

It is because we regard the affirmations of Engels and Garaudy as *directive principles*, indications of tasks and problems, and not as concrete truths. *They do not at this stage constitute knowledge—everything remains to be done, we have still to find a method and constitute a science.*

The misapplication of these directive principles to a situation to give a spurious *a priori* knowledge which does not draw its concepts from experience is illustrated by Lukács's thesis that Heidegger's existentialism transformed itself into an activism under the influence of the Nazis, while French existentialism, liberal and antifascist, expresses the revolt of a petite bourgeoisie oppressed during the German occupation. This imposed scheme is invalidated by Sartre in a fine piece of ironic writing. At least one current of German existentialism refused all collusion with the Nazis and survived—namely Jaspers: Sartre's *L'Être et le Néant* resulted from researches undertaken by him in 1933 in Berlin under the influence of Husserl, Scheler, and Heidegger—that is at a time when Heidegger was presumably in a state of full 'activism': Sartre had worked out the method and principal conclusions of his book in the winter of 1939-40 prior to his Occupation experience: Heidegger has never been activist in his writings. Sartre advises Lukács actually to read Heidegger and study him sentence by sentence—although he says he knows no Marxist capable of this. There is a whole dialectic, and a very complex one, from Brentano to Husserl to Heidegger. This constitutes what Sartre calls a 'regional history' and cannot be dismissed as a pure epiphenomenon.

Can we not consider Husserl's phenomenology as a moment conserved and depassed by Heidegger's system? This requires no change in the principles of Marxism, but the situation becomes much more complex. If the situation is complex one may have regrets, but one must accept it in its complexity.

Sartre characterizes the bad faith that besets contemporary Marxists as their concealment from themselves of their resort to teleological explanations. So many Marxist explanations define the historical enterprise being studied by the end results to which it leads, or often the enterprise is reduced to the propagation of a physical motion in a setting of inertia. To think, for most of these Marxists, is to pretend to totalize. What really happens is that the particular is replaced by a universal. There is a pretended process of leading on to the concrete, but in fact this amounts to the presentation of determinations which are fundamental but abstract. Hegel at least allowed the particular to subsist as a depassed particular, but Marxists now feel that they would be wasting their time if they were to try to comprehend a form of bourgeois thought in its *originality*. For them it is simply a matter of reducing it to a mode of idealism which is proposed as a concrete reality. For them the being of bourgeois thought is its permanent reducibility to an *idealism-substance*—whereas in itself it is essentially lack of substance. From this springs a perpetual fetishization.

However, it is a Marxist, Henri Lefebvre,[1] who gives us a method for integrating history and sociology in the perspective

[1] Henri Lefebvre: 'Perspectives de sociologie rurale', *Cahiers de Sociologie*, 1953.

of dialectical materialism which Sartre finds irreproachable. Lefebvre notes that in studying, for example, the reality of a peasantry there is first of all a *horizontal complexity* which concerns a human group with its agricultural productive techniques, its relation to these techniques and the social structure they determine which in turn conditions the group. The group depends on collectivities on the national and international scale, and so on. Then there is a *vertical complexity* which is historical, the co-existence in the rural world of formations of different age and duration. These two complexities act and react on each other. To study such a situation preserving its full complexity Lefebvre delineates a method with three moments. *First*: a phase of phenomenological description—observation informed by experience and by a general theory. *Second*: an analytico-regressive moment—a regression backward into the history of the object to define and date its earlier stages. *Third*: A synthetic progressive moment which is still historico-genetic but moves from past to present in an attempt to rediscover the present, as elucidated and reconstituted in the light of the complete phenomenological analytico-synthetic regressive-progressive procedure.

Sartre holds this method to be valid, with modifications, for all the domains of anthropology,[1] and applies it later also to individuals and concrete relations between individuals.

If we wish to understand, say, Valéry, an intellectual coming from the concrete historical group of the French petite bourgeoisie at the end of the last century, then we should not go to the Marxists. They would substitute for this well-defined group the *idea* of its material conditions and its relations with other groups and its internal contradictions. We return thus to economic categories and see the oscillations of the social attitude of the petite bourgeoisie in terms of its simultaneous threat from capitalist concentration on the one hand and popular revenge on the other.

---

[1] Anthropology here should be understood in the wider Continental sense of a general theory of man and the human condition and not in the sense of such specific disciplines as physical and cultural anthropology and ethnology.

This skeleton of unversality is quite true *on its level of abstraction*. But we are concerned with Valéry, a *particular man*.

All the characteristics of Valéry's thought are determined dialectically in relation to the Marxist's materialism, which is always presented as the independent variable that never itself submits to or depends on other thought. At a certain point the abstract schematization ceases and the Marxist judges his work finished. As for Valéry, he has evaporated.

We also, Sartre says, pretend that idealism is an object because we name it, teach and accept or combat it. It was a living philosophy and is now a dead one. It bore witness to certain relations between men. We do not, however, see it as a thing but as an idea-object—a special type of reality. It has real presence and historical depth. Valéry's ideology should be seen as the concrete, singular product of a being who characterizes himself partly by his relation to idealism, but who must be deciphered in his particularity, starting with the concrete group from which he came.

Undoubtedly he is a petit-bourgeois intellectual, but every petit-bourgeois intellectual is not Valéry, and this sums up the heuristic deficiency of contemporary Marxism.

What is lacking in Marxism is a *hierarchy of mediations* which is necessary to grasp the process by which a person and his product are produced in the interior of a given class and society at a given historical moment. In writing of Valéry and his idealistic work, the Marxist finds in both only that which he himself has put there. This leads to his eliminating the particular by defining it as the simple effect of chance. As Engels says, if Napoleon had not existed another would have been there to fill his place. Existentialism, on the other hand, insists on discovering mediations in order to grasp the concrete singular individual.

Present-day Marxists show Flaubert's realism in a reciprocal relation with the social and political evolution of the petite bourgeoisie of the Second Empire. But it does not show the genesis of this reciprocity, nor why Flaubert preferred literature above all, nor why he wrote those particular books rather than the books of, say, the Goncourts. This Marxism leaves to other disciplines which lack fundamental principles. Marxism has nothing to say about this all-important phrase: 'to belong to the bourgeoisie'. Children are not born at the age when they earn their first wages or own their capital and exploit their first worker. The child does not experience his alienation and reification first of all in the course of his own work but in the course of the work of his parents. It was not rent from property nor the intellectual nature of his work that made Flaubert belong to the bourgeoisie, but the fact that he was born into a family which was already bourgeois. He accepted the roles and gestures imposed upon him at a time when he could not comprehend their meaning. But, like all families, that of Flaubert was a particular family, and it was in the face of the particular contradictions of this family that Flaubert served his apprenticeship as a bourgeois. No change was involved. He lived, in its particularity, the conflict between the reviving religious pomp of a monarchist régime and the agnosticism of his father who was a petit-bourgeois child of the revolution.

Today only psycho-analysis allows us to study the process whereby a child, groping in the dark, tries at first to play the role which is imposed upon him by his parents. Psycho-analysis alone shows us whether the child evades this role, whether it proves fatal for him, or whether he assimilates it entirely. It alone allows us to find in the adult the whole man, with the full weight of his history. It would be quite wrong to see this discipline as opposed to dialectical materialism, although admittedly some incautious psycho-analysts have put forward theories of society and of history which end in idealism. Marxism can no longer do without the mediation which would enable it to pass from abstract, general determinations to the singular individual.

Psycho-analysis lacks principles and a theoretical basis and it is quite fitting that, in Jung, and in certain works of Freud, it resorts to a perfectly inoffensive mythology. In fact, psycho-analysis is a method preoccupied above all else with establishing the manner in which the child lives his family relations in the interior of a given society. This by no means places in doubt the priority of institutions; quite on the contrary, the child's family, as this particular family, is only the singularization of the family structure proper to *this* particular class under *these* conditions.

Unlike Marxism in its present state, existentialism can accord psycho-analysis its correct place. Psycho-analysis discovers the point of insertion of a man in his class. It discovers, that is to say, the particular family as mediation between the universal class and the individual. The family is constituted in and through the general movement of history and in the depth and opacity of each particular childhood it is lived as an absolute.

Sartre reassures Marxists that they have nothing to fear in the new methods of psycho-analysis and existentialism which aim simply to reinstate concrete regions of the real. The illnesses of the person take on their true meaning when they are seen as the concrete translation of the alienation of man. Existentialism assisted by psycho-analysis can today only study those situations where man has lost himself since infancy, for in a society founded on exploitation there are no other situations.

Each of us lives his first years in a state of wandering and groping, and here the interiorization of exteriority is an irreducible fact. Psycho-analysis, in the interior of a dialectical totalization, meets, on the one hand, objective structures, material conditions, and, on the other, the action of our indepassable childhood on our adult life. It is henceforth impossible to relate Madame Bovary directly to the politico-social structure and the evolution of the petite bourgeoisie. The work must be related to a present reality lived by Flaubert throughout his childhood.

The Marxist view that the social actions of a person are conditioned by the general interests of his class is by no means incompatible with the idea of the conditioning of present action by infantile experience. Most of us have not outgrown the prejudices, beliefs, and ideas of our childhood: our irrational reactions spring from our blindness in infancy—from the prolonged madness of early life. But, Sartre asks, what is this indepassable childhood if not a particular mode of living the general interests of the environment?

Sartre considers certain types of sociology. The principles of these sociologies often constitute a masked idealism. Lewin, for example, makes a fetish of totalization—instead of seeing the real movement of history he hypostatizes it into totalities-already-made. There is a synthesis of exteriority whereby the sociologist remains exterior to this given totality. Sociology opposes itself to Marxism not in so far as it affirms the provisional autonomy of its method—which in fact gives us the means to integrate it—but in affirming the radical autonomy of its object in three respects. In the first place, *ontological autonomy*: despite all precautions, the group thus conceived becomes a substantial unity—*even and especially if* one defines its existence by its simple functioning; in the second place, *methodological autonomy*: the substitution of actual, completed totalities for dialectical movement. A science based on structural laws concerned with function, or functional relations between the parts of a whole, can study what Lefebvre calls horizontal complexity. It cannot study the history of the individual or that of the group. Then, in the third place, there is *reciprocal autonomy* of the experimenter and the experimental group. The sociologist is either not situated or if he is he takes precautions to desituate himself. He may provisionally integrate himself in the group but only in the knowledge that he will later disengage himself.

In fact, the sociologist and his 'object' form a couple in which each is interpreted by the other and of which the relation itself must be deciphered as a moment of history.

Still, sociology as it exists at present, as a provisional moment of historical totalization, with its absence of theoretical foundation and with the precision of its auxiliary methods—tests, statistics, and so on—reveals new mediations between concrete persons and the material conditions of their life, between human relations and relations of production, between persons and classes (or any other form of group).

The group, for Sartre, has not and cannot have the type of metaphysical existence which some sociologists wish to give it. In accord with Marxism, Sartre holds that, as far as groups are concerned, there are only men and real relations between men. The group is nothing but a multiplicity of relations and relations between relations. This certitude derives from our consideration of the relation of the sociologist and his object as a relation of reciprocity—the investigator can never be 'outside' the group except to the extent to which he is 'in' another group—except in those limited cases where this 'exile' from the group is the consequence of a real *act* of exclusion.

Sartre goes on to state the theme developed further in the *Critique* that the reality of collective objects of study consists in *recurrence*. This recurrence shows that totalization is never achieved and that totality never exists as more than a detotalized totality. These collectives exist in such a way that they reveal themselves immediately to action and to perception. We shall always find in each of them a concrete materiality (movement, buildings, words, and so on) which sustains and manifests a process which erodes it.

It is not a question of adding another method to Marxism. The very development of dialectical philosophy should produce, in a single act of synthesis, a totalization both horizontal and vertical. Sartre warns that if Marxism refuses to do this others will attempt it.

From the day when Marxist research will take the human dimension (i.e. the existential project) as the foundation for anthropological knowledge, existentialism will no longer have a *raison d'être*. Absorbed and conserved, that is depassed, by the totalizing movement of philosophy, it will cease to be a particular inquiry and become the foundation of all inquiry. Sartre's statements in this essay aim at hastening the moment of this dissolution.

48

III. THE PROGRESSIVE-REGRESSIVE METHOD

Sartre accepts without reservations the thesis of Engels that 'men make their history themselves but in a given environment which conditions them'. This thesis, however, is open to many different interpretations. Idealistic Marxism seems to have chosen the easiest interpretation, namely that man is a passive product, a bundle of conditioned reflexes, entirely determined by anterior circumstances which in the last analysis are economic conditions. This inert object somehow inserts itself into the social order along with other similarly conditioned objects, and, through its received nature, hastens or slows down the development of the world. It changes society in the same way that a bomb, obeying the principle of inertia, destroys a city. On this view there is no difference between man and a machine.

If, however, we wish to do justice to what Sartre regards as the correct Marxist position, we must say that man, in a period of exploitation, is, at one and the same time, the product of his own product *and* a historical agent who cannot be considered as a product. This is not a static contradiction but has to be grasped in the very movement of praxis. Then it will illuminate Engels's statement: men make their history on the basis of real anterior conditions (acquired characters, distortions imposed by the mode of work and of life, alienation, etc.), *but it is they, the men, who make history and not the anterior conditions*. Otherwise they would be simply the vehicles of inhuman forces. Of course the anterior conditions exist and it is these alone which can provide a direction and a material reality for the changes which take place. But the movement of human praxis depasses these conditions while conserving them.

It is true that the real effects of men's actions often escape them. The proletariat as historical subject does not necessarily in a single movement realize at all clearly its unity and become fully conscious of its historical role. But if my history escapes me this does not mean that I do not make my history. It 'escapes me' because *the others also* make history.

Marx put his thought in very precise terms. If, for example one wishes to act on or influence (*agir*) an educator, then one must act on or modify the factors which condition him. In Marxist thought we find inseparably linked the characters of external determination and those of the progressive synthetic unity which is human praxis. The most profound level of Marxist theorizing concerns this will to transcend the oppositions of exteriority and interiority, multiplicity and unity, analysis and synthesis, nature and antiphysis. But, Sartre says, these are only indications which must be developed and it would be a grave error to regard this task as an easy one.

Sartre develops the notion of the historical subject by examining Engels's account of the Peasant War in Germany. The lack of unity of the numerous provincial peasant movements resulted in each group lacking a real sense of *enterprise*. The results of the local peasant movements may have appeared successful when viewed from the local perspective, but within the framework of a totalization their effect was radically different. Man makes history. That is, he objectifies and alienates himself in it. History is the work (*œuvre*) of *all* the activity of *all* men and it appears as an alien force to them exactly to the extent to which they do not recognize the meaning of their enterprise in the objective total result (even if their enterprise achieves some *local* success). In making separate truces the peasants in a certain province won a local victory but thereby weakened their class, and this latter effect then turned against them.

In becoming conscious of itself, the proletariat becomes an historical subject, that is to say the proletariat recognizes itself in history. Through the unification of the exploited and the reduction in number of the conflicting classes, history finally will have meaning for men. But we are not yet at this point. There are proletariats (in the plural), there are differently developing national proletariats. It would, however, be as wrong to fail to appreciate the solidarity of these proletariats as to underestimate their separation. It is true that divisions and their theoretical consequences, namely the decay of bourgeois ideology and the temporary arrest of Marxism, oblige our epoch to make itself without knowing itself, but it is not true that history is completely an alien force to us.

The present plurality of meaning of history means that history can only discover itself and pose itself for itself on the basis of a future totalization, as a function of this future totalization, and in contradiction to it. It is our daily duty to come nearer to this totalization. All remains obscure and yet all is in full daylight. We have the theoretical instruments and we can establish a method. Our historical task at the heart of this polyvalent world is to come nearer and nearer to the moment when, in a sense, history will have only one total meaning: the moment when history will become dissolved into concrete *men* who will make it together.

The Project

Alienation can modify the results of an action but not its profound reality. We refuse to confuse the alienated man with a thing, or alienation with physical laws. We affirm the specificity of the human act which penetrates the social environment transforming the world on the basis of given conditions. Man is characterized above all else by the depassment of a situation, because he is able to *do* or *undo* what has been *done to* him, even if he never recognizes himself in his objectification. We find this depassment at the root of what is human and first of all we find it in need (*besoin*). Among the Marquesans, for example, this is what links together the scarcity of women as a structural fact of the group with the matrimonial institution of polyandry. This scarcity is not a simple organic lack. Even in its most naked form it is a social situation and contains within itself an effort of depassment. The most rudimentary conduct must be determined at one and the same time in relation to real, present factors which condition it and in relation to a certain future object to which it attempts to give birth. This is what we call *the project*. A double simultaneous relation can be defined: in relation to the given, praxis is negativity, but it always involves also the negation of a negation; in relation to the object at which we aim, it is positivity, but this positivity opens out onto the non-existent, that which is not yet. The project is both negation and realization: it retains and unveils the depassed which it has negated in its very movement of depassment. Knowledge is thus a moment of praxis, even the most rudimentary praxis, but this knowledge has nothing to do with absolute Knowing. This knowledge is defined by the negation of the reality which is refused in the name of the reality which is yet to be produced. It remains captive to the action which it illuminates and disappears along with this action. It is perfectly true, then, that man is the product of his product; the structures of a society created by human labour define for each one of us an objective point of departure. It might be asserted that the truth of a man is the nature of his work and his wages, but this nature is perpetually depassed by the man in his praxis. This depassment is only conceivable as the relation of an existent to his possibilities. The material conditions of a man's life circumscribe his field of possibilities, e.g. if he is too fatigued by his work he cannot be active in his trade union. The field of his possibilities is that goal towards which a man moves in depassing his objective situation. The field of possibilities in its turn is strictly dependent on the social and historical reality. To say what a man *is* is to say at the same time that which he *can be*, and conversely.

However reduced it might be, a field of possibilities always remains before man. This field should not be regarded as a zone of indetermination but, on the contrary, as a well-structured region, which depends on history in its entirety and which contains its own contradictions. It is in depassing the given towards the field of possibilities and in realizing one possibility amongst all the possibilities, that the individual objectifies himself and contributes to the making of history. The agent's project then assumes a reality, *which the agent himself may not know*, but which, by the conflicts it manifests and which give rise to it, influences the course of events. Possibility must be conceived of as doubly determined. On the one hand, it is at the heart of the particular action as the presence of the future as that which is lacking, and that which unveils reality by this very absence. On the other hand, it has a more positive sense as the real, permanent future which ceaselessly maintains and transforms the collective. As well as positively defining possibilities, every man is defined negatively by that collection of possibilities which are impossible for him, that is, by a future which is more or less closed. Positively and negatively, social possibilities are experienced as schematic determinants of the individual future. The most individual possibility is nothing more than the interiorization and enrichment of a social possibility.

Marxists cannot be excused their mechanistic materialism when one considers their knowledge of and approval of the immense socialist plans. For a Chinese the future is more true than the present. If one has not studied the 'structures of the future' of a determined society one has understood nothing of its sociality.

Sartre says that he cannot consider here the true dialectic of the subjective and the objective. It would be necessary to show the conjoint necessity of the 'interiorization of the exterior' and the 'exteriorization of the interior'. Praxis, in effect, is the passage *from* the objective through interiorization *to* the objective. The project, as subjective depassment of objectivity towards objectivity, is stretched between the objective conditions of the environment and the objective structures of the field of possibilities. It represents in itself the moving unity of subjectivity and objectivity, these cardinal moments of activity. The subjective appears as a necessary moment of the objective process, the objective as a necessary moment of subjectivity.

Whatever examples we take, we shall find that objective processes always refer to an experienced reality. A decrease in purchasing power never provokes workers to revenge unless they experience a need in their flesh. The worker in this example knows what he experiences and what other workers will be experiencing. But to experience is already to depass the given towards the possibility of its objective transformation. In lived experience subjectivity eliminates itself as pure subjectivity and extricates itself from despair by objectification. Thus subjectivity holds within itself the objectivity which it negates and depasses towards a new objectivity, and this new objectivity, as objectification, exteriorizes the interiority of the project as an objectified subjectivity. That is to say, the experienced as such finds its place in the result (the objectified subjectivity) and the projected meaning of the action appears in the reality of the world to assume its truth in the process of totalization. Only the project as mediation between two moments of objectivity can account for history, that is, for human creativity.

Sartre undertakes to formulate the problem of the dialectical temporality of history and to point out its difficulties. Because of its failure to develop itself in real investigations, Marxism uses an arrested dialectic which operates the totalization of human activities within an infinitely divisible homogeneous continuum that is nothing more or less than the time of Cartesian rationalism. This temporality-milieu is not out of place when one examines the processes of capital since it is just this sort of temporality which is produced by the capitalist economy as the meaning of production, monetary circulation, credit, and so on. But this description is one thing and the dialectical determination of real temporality is another (real temporality, that is to say, which concerns the true relation of men to their past and to their future). The dialectic as movement of reality dissolves away if time is not dialectical— that is to say if one refuses the future as such to a certain action. Neither men nor their activities are *in* time but men create time, as a concrete characteristic of history, on the basis of their original temporalization. Marxism began to grasp true temporality when it criticized bourgeois notions of progress—which necessarily imply a homogeneous milieu and fixed co-ordinates which permit one to 'situate' a point of departure and a point of arrival. But

Marxism itself, without saying so openly, renounced these critical researches, preferring to substitute its own notions of progress.

We have to choose: either we reduce all to identity (in which case dialectical materialism is transformed into mechanical materialism), or we make the dialectic a celestial law which imposes itself on the universe, a metaphysical force which generates the historical process from within itself (Hegelian idealism), or we credit the individual man with his capacity to depass his situation by work and action. Only the latter position enables us to ground the movement of totalization in reality. We must search for the dialectic in the relations between man and nature, in the 'conditions of departure', and in the relations between man and man. It is there that it has its source as the resultant of the meeting-point of projects. The development of these considerations belongs to the *Critique* and in the *Questions* Sartre limits himself to outlining three observations which should help us see this exposition as a summary problematic (*problematique sommaire*) of existentialism.

1. The given which we depass every instant that we live, by the simple fact that we live it, is not reducible to the material conditions of our existence. *We depass also our infancy and childhood.* In childhood we dimly apprehended our class and our social conditioning through our experience of the family group: as children we make a more or less blind attempt to depass this. This experience coupled with our effort to snatch ourselves away from it finally ended in inscribing itself on us as a *character*. It is on this level that we learn the gestures of a bourgeois or of a socialist and the contradictory roles which compress us and tear us apart (e.g. Flaubert's role of the pious, day-dreaming child and his role as the doctor, son of an atheist doctor). On this level also are the traces of early revolts and attempted depassments of a suffocating reality, and the various twists and deviations which result from this. But to depass these things is also to preserve them—we think *with* these early deviations, we act *with* the learned gestures

from which we wish to turn away. In projecting ourselves towards our possibilities to escape the contradiction of our existence, we unveil these contradictions, they are revealed in our very actions, even if the actions are richer than them and lead us to a social world in which new contradictions lead us to new forms of conduct. Thus, simultaneously, we ceaselessly depass our class *and* this very depassment manifests our class reality to us. The realization of a possibility leads to the production of an object or of an event in the social world, and it is thus that our objectification and early contradictions reflected there bear witness to our alienation.

What contemporary Marxists forget is that the man who is alienated, mystified, reified, and so on, remains none the less a man. When Marx writes of reification he does not mean to show us that we have been transformed into things, but that we are men condemned to live humanly the condition of material things.

If we examine miserliness or meanness, which is common in certain sections of the French bourgeoisie, we would miss the concrete reality if we saw the miserly person as the simple result of a Malthusian economics, for stinginess originates in infancy when the child scarcely knows what money is, because stinginess is also a defiant mode of living his own body and his position in the world, and it bears a relation to death. We must study such concrete characteristics *on the basis of* economic movement but without failing to understand their *specificity*. Only in this way can we aim at totalization.

We must remember also that we live our childhood *as our future*. Our gestures and roles are taught and learned in the perspective of that-which-is-to-come. They are inseparable from the project which transforms them. Depassed and yet retained, they constitute what Sartre calls the *internal colouration of the project*. The motivation is the 'why' of the project and the specification of the project is the 'what'. Motivation and specification form a single reality which is the project. The project never has a content

56

since its objectives simultaneously are united to it and transcend it.

But the colouration of the project, that is to say subjectively its taste or flavour and objectively its style, is nothing other than the depassment of our early deviations—this depassment being not an instantaneous movement but a protracted labour. Each moment of this labour is at once a depassment and, to the extent to which it poses itself for itself, the pure and simple subsisting of these early deviations on a given level of integration. For this reason a person's life unrolls itself in spirals. It repeatedly passes by the same points, but on different levels of integration and complexity.

To take an example: Flaubert as a child felt frustrated by his older brother in gaining his father's affection. His brother Achille resembled the father, and in order to please the father the young Flaubert would have to imitate Achille—which he refused to do in resentment and sulkiness. The same situation was repeated at the university—where Achille nine years earlier had obtained top marks, in order to please the professor of medicine who had himself been a brilliant student. Flaubert again would have had to repeat all his brother's acts and in an unformulated way he refused to do this. He resisted success and would become only a good enough student—which was a dishonour in the Flaubert family. His family problem was so serious for Flaubert that it dominated his relations with his fellow-students. If he felt humiliated by his fellow-students' successes this was only because they confirmed the superiority of Achille. The third moment again is an enrichment and rearrangement of the original situation—here Flaubert decided that, to be sure of being *different* from Achille he would be *inferior* to him. He detested his future career as a proof of his inferiority and had hysterical crises. This movement from early childhood to hysterical crisis was not simple repetition but a perpetual depassment of the given which led finally to Flaubert's literary engagement. We have been dealing all the time here with the past as depassed (*passé—dépassé*) but at the same time with the past as depassing (*passé—dépassant*) that is to say as *future*. Our roles are always *future* structures. They are tasks to be carried out, traps to be avoided and so on.

Complexes, style of life, and the revealing of the past as depassing, as a future to be created, constitute one and the same reality. It is the project as orientated life, as the affirmation of man by action, but it is at the same time this fog of unlocatable irrationality lying between our reciprocally reflecting early memories and rational adult choices. Sartre says that it is necessary to state the perspective when he talks of irrationality. He means *irrationality for us* and *not* irrationality in itself. He also admits to being outrageously schematic in relation to Flaubert's complex real problems—his sole intention being to show the persistent motives and intentions present in his various transformations.

The totalization must discover the multidimensional unity of the act—our old habits of thought and the present state of language are not well fitted to give an account of this unity. Dialectical knowledge of man since Hegel and Marx needs a new rationality. For want of having constructed such a rationality, every word written and said about us both in the East and in the West can be nothing but a gross error. Sartre qualifies this apparently sweeping statement in a footnote, however, when he says that even errors contain bits of real knowledge.

2. If we wish to study Flaubert, who is presented in books on literature as the father of realism, we learn that he said 'Madame Bovary, It is I'. We discover that his most subtle contemporaries, above all Baudelaire, had earlier guessed this identification.

We learn that the father of realism, during his voyage in the Orient, dreamed of writing the story of a mystical virgin in the Low Countries who was the symbol of his own cult of Art. Finally, going to his biography we discover his dependence, his obedience, and his 'relative being' (*être relatif*), in fact all the characteristics which we are now accustomed to call *feminine*. It seems, further, that his doctors treated him as a nervous old woman and that he felt vaguely flattered by this. For all that he is undoubtedly not in any degree a homosexual. His letters to Louise Colet show him to be a narcissist and a masturbator, but he also boasts of amorous adventures which were probably true, as he was addressing himself to the only person who could be both witness and judge.

Without leaving the work, we shall thus be concerned with asking why the author (that is to say, the pure synthetic activity from which issued *Madame Bovary*) transformed himself into woman. What significance does this metamorphosis have *in itself*? This presupposes a phenomenological study of Emma Bovary in the book. We then go on to ask *who* must Flaubert have been that, in the field of his possibilities, he should have had the possibility of portraying himself as a woman?

Sartre proceeds to make the important statement that the answer to these questions is independent of all biography, since the question could be posed in Kantian terms: 'what are the conditions of the possibility of the feminization of experience?'

To reply to this question we should never forget that an author's style is directly linked to a certain conception of the world. The structure of his phrases, paragraphs, his usage of substantives and verbs, and so on, all these particularities of style translate secret presuppositions which we can determine differentially without yet having recourse to the biography. Still we only arrive at problems.

It is true that the intentions of his contemporaries assist us here: Baudelaire affirmed the identity of the deeper meaning of, on the one hand, the *Temptation of Saint Anthony* in which there is a complete confusion of the grand metaphysical themes of the age (the destiny of man, life, death, God, religion, nothingness, etc.) and, on the other, of *Madame Bovary*, a work which (in appearance at least) is dry and objective. *Who* could and must Flaubert have been to have expressed his own reality in the form of an insane idealism *and* a realism which is more wicked than impassive? Who could and must Flaubert have been to have objectified himself in works some years apart as a mystical monk and as a determined and somewhat masculine woman?

To continue our analysis beyond this point we must resort to biography, that is to say, to facts collected by his contemporaries and verified by the historians. Flaubert's work prompts questions about his life. But we have to understand in what sense his work, as objectification of the person, is in effect more complete, more total than his life. Certainly it has its roots in his life and illuminates it, but it finds its total explanation only in itself. However, it is still too soon for this explanation to appear to us. Flaubert's life is illuminated (*éclairé*) by his work as a reality whose total determination is found outside itself, at once in the conditions that produce it and in the artistic creation it achieves.

Thus the work, when we have paged through it, *becomes both hypothesis and research method* to illuminate the life history: it interrogates concrete episodes in the life history and retains them as answers to its questions. But these answers are not enough. They are limited to the extent to which objectification in art is not reducible to objectivation in everyday conduct. There is a gap between the work and the life. The man and his relationships thus illuminated appear to us as a synthetic ensemble of questions. The works of Flaubert reveal his narcissism, his onanism, his idealism, his passivity, and so on, but these characteristics in their turn are problems for us. These regressive questions provide us with the means to examine his family group as a reality lived and overcome by the child, aided by a double source of information— on the one hand, objective evidence about the family, its class characteristics and its individual peculiarities, and, on the other, the violently subjective judgements on it by Flaubert. In this sense we must continually turn to the works of the author, realizing that they contain biographical truth which is not found in his correspondence, which is full of his distortions, but one must also realize that the works never reveal the secrets of the biography, they can be only the schema which permits us to discover these secrets in the life itself.

These regressive facts show the traces of a dialectical movement, not the movement itself. It is only at this point, however, that we are able to use the progressive method. What we have to discover is the enriching movement of totalization which delivers each moment from its antecedent moment, the movement which passes from the early obscurities lived by the child to his final objectification of himself in the world. This in fact is the project by which Flaubert, in order to escape from the petite bourgeoisie, threaded his way through the various fields of possibilities towards the alienated objectification of himself as the author of *Madame Bovary* and as this petit bourgeois whom he refused to be. This project is not a simple negativity, a flight. By the project the subject 'produces' himself in the world as an objective totality. Flaubert's choice was not the simple abstract choice to write, but to write in a certain manner so as to manifest himself in the world in a certain way. His project is the singular signification which he gave to literature as the negation of his original condition and as the objective solution of his contradictions. We have a series of signifying traces from the material and social conditioning to the work, and we must discover the tension between one objectification and the other. We have to invent a movement, or re-create it, but our hypothesis is immediately verifiable—to be valid it must realize, in a creative movement, the transversal unity of *all* the heterogeneous structures.

Sartre goes on to define the methodological approach of existentialism as a regressive-progressive and analytico-synthetic method. It is an enriching reciprocal movement between the object (which contains the whole epoch as hierarchized significations) and the epoch (which contains the object within its totalization). Further, when the object is rediscovered in its depth and singularity, instead of remaining exterior to the totalization it immediately enters into contradiction with it. The simple and inert juxtaposition of object and epoch is replaced by a living conflict.

3. A man defines himself by his project. The true structure of a life is this immediate relation, beyond the given and the constituted, with the other-than-self: this ceaseless production of self by work and praxis. It is not a need or a feeling, but our needs, feelings, and even our most abstract thoughts participate in it. They are in a perpetual state of being-beyond-themselves-towards. This is what we call existence, and by this term we clearly do not mean a stable substance reposing within itself but a perpetual disequilibrium. Since this impulse towards objectification takes on diverse forms according to the individual, and since it impels us through a field of possibilities of which we realize some to the exclusion of others, we also call it choice or freedom. It would, however, be a mistake to see this as an introduction of the irrational or of a fetishized freedom detached from the world. Such a reproach could be addressed only from the standpoint of a mechanistic philosophy which would reduce praxis, creation, and invention to the elementary givens of a life, that is to say, a philosophy which would *explain* the works or the attitudes of a person by the factors which *condition* them. This approach is a covert attempt to reduce the complex to the simple, to deny the specificity of things, and to reduce change to identity. The dialectical method is aimed at something completely opposite to this reduction. Its movement is one of depassment implying a conservation, but the contradictory terms which have been depassed can account for neither the depassment itself nor the further synthesis. On the contrary, it is the latter which illuminates the contradictions and enables us to understand them. What we have to examine and question is the choice which gives a life uniqueness. By his choice to write, Flaubert disclosed to us the meaning of his childhood fear of death—and not the reverse. Man constructs signs as the being who in his very being is the dialectical depassment of the simply given. The irreducibility of the cultural order to the natural order is entailed by the notion of freedom that Sartre develops.

To grasp the meaning of any human conduct we must use what

psychiatrists and historians in Germany have called 'comprehension'. This does not denote some special gift or intuitive faculty. This type of knowledge is simply the dialectical movement which explains the act by its final signification departing from its original condition.

Sartre gives the following example of comprehension: I am working with a friend in a room which has become hot and stuffy. On the basis of the material conditions in the room, I comprehend the actions of my friend who gets up and walks towards the window. His actions are not implicit in the material conditions, nor are they released by or provoked by these conditions. We are concerned here with a synthetic conduct which unifies the practical field in the room in unifying itself. My friend adapts his movements to the particular circumstances, such as the disposition of furniture in the room. To depass the succession of gestures towards the unity which they achieve, it is necessary for me to experience the stuffy atmosphere in the room as the lived depassment of the original situation. In the room the door and windows are not completely passive realities. Work by men has given them specific instrumental meanings, and I comprehend these meanings. My friend's behaviour discloses the practical field as a 'hodological space' and, conversely, indications implicit in the material objects become the crystallized meaning which permits me to comprehend his enterprise. My friend's behaviour unifies the interior of the room and the room defines his behaviour. The movement of comprehension is simultaneously progressive (towards the objective result) and regressive (returning to the original condition). Comprehension is nothing other than my real life, that is to say, the totalizing movement which gathers together myself, the other person, and the environment in the synthetic unity of an objectification in process. Significations in the environment or in the other never appear to us except in so far as we ourselves are signifying beings. Our comprehension of the other is never contemplative, it is a moment of our praxis, a mode of living. Whether by conflict or by its suppression, it is the concrete human relation that unites us to the other.

Any simple observation of the social field should make us realize that the relation to ends is a universal structure of human enterprises and that it is on the basis of this relation that men understand actions and institutions. Comprehension of the other is achieved only through a realization of the ends of his acts and projects. One may watch a man working from a distance and feel that one does not comprehend what he is doing, until one realizes the end at which he is aiming in his labour so that all his different movements become unified in the light of the end. Ends are not mysterious entities or some sort of appendages to acts. They simply represent the depassment of the given in an act which passes from the present to the future.

2. SARTRE ON GENET

Jean Genet—bastard, vagabond, pederast, thief, outcast, dramatist, poet—is the subject of the most extended application of these ideas to a life-history. In his book, *Saint Genet, Comédien et Martyr*, Sartre seeks to show that only through a consideration of the dialectic of freedom acting under given material conditions can the concrete reality of a man's life be grasped. He shows a particular freedom at grips with destiny, at first apparently crushed and suffocated by fatedness, later eroding this fatedness piece by piece. If Genet is a genius, then his genius is not a God- or gene-given gift, but an issue invented by Genet alone, in particular moments of despair. He seeks to rediscover the choice which Genet makes of himself, his life, and the meaning of the world, to become a writer, and to show how the unique specificity of this choice pervades even the interstices of the formal character of Genet's style, the structure of his images, and the particularity of his tastes. He aims, in a word, to retrace in rigorous detail 'the story of a liberation'.

Sartre has undertaken his biography equipped with an intimate knowledge of all Genet's texts, and with a background of a personal relationship with Genet himself. Contrary to certain critical opinions which have been proffered, we believe that Sartre does succeed in conveying a radical understanding of Genet as a living whole, while also evoking for the reader Genet as a real presence. Sartre appears to have been fascinated by Genet, and the reader finds this fascination contagious, even through pages of the most formidable dialectic. Sartre, indeed, explores the complex feelings of fascination invoked in him by Genet and uses them to understand his subject.

The skeletal facts of Genet's life are that he was born in Paris in 1910 and abandoned by his mother to the Assistance Publique. He was 'illegitimate', and never knew his parents. He was adopted by a peasant family in the Morvan and at the age of 10, after having been caught stealing from them on various occasions, he was sent to a reformatory at Mettray. He spent some years in this type of institution, and then escaped to join the Foreign Legion, which he soon deserted. As a vagabond and thief he wandered through Europe, spending some time in the prisons of various countries. While in prison in 1942, he wrote his first book, *Notre-Dame des Fleurs*, followed during the next five years by novels, plays, and poems. In 1948, after ten convictions for theft in France, he escaped life imprisonment when pardoned by the President of the Republic, who had been petitioned by a number of eminent writers and artists, including Cocteau, Picasso, and Sartre himself.

In ten years of writing, in Sartre's view, Genet achieved something of the equivalent of a psycho-analytic cure. Each of his books represents a crisis of katharsis, each is a psychodrama, each reproduces the theme of its predecessors—as his new love-affairs reproduce his old loves—each makes him a little more master of the demon which possesses him. We now turn to Sartre's account of Genet's childhood.

During his first years in the country, in the Morvan, Genet lived in what Sartre calls 'a sweet confusion with the world'. His existence was scattered amongst nature. Caressed by the wild grass and water, he was in a state of innocence. He grew up piously, a gentle and respectful child, smaller and weaker than his playmates, but more intelligent. The curé felt he had a religious nature, but Genet was already the victim of a cruel mystification. This myth of childhood innocence, the state of original grace, in which he was submerged, rings false, and could not be sustained, for Genet was a false child. With no real mother of his own, with no heritage, he belonged to no one, and no one and nothing belonged to him. His mere existence disturbed the social order. An Institution with its register of names and its bureaucracy was interposed between Genet and the human race. Certainly he was born of a woman, but this physical origin was not retained in the collective memory. He came into the world from an unknown womb, almost as an article produced by a modern factory bears no trace of the human producer. Belonging originally to an administrative apparatus, his later affinities tended to be for institutions— the reformatory and the prison.

From his earliest years, the unknown mother was one of the principal figures in Genet's mythology. To him the reformatory at Mettray was, in a sense, his mother. The colony appeared 'with all that which is peculiar to woman, tenderness, the queasy eructation from a half-open mouth, the deep breast lifted by a swelling movement, finally with all that which makes a mother Mother'.[1] Genet's later experiences of rejection by society are found in germinal form in his feeling of rejection by his own mother and by his adoptive family. When he tries to find his true origins beyond the bureaucracy of which he appears to be an emanation, Genet finds that his birth coincides with a gesture of refusal. In his phantasies as a child, the woman tore him from herself, a living, bleeding part of herself, and threw him out of and beyond the world. He had been cursed forever. From that time forth he was the unloved, the inopportune, the supernumerary. Genet felt himself to be undesirable in his very being, not the son of this woman, but her excrement. For Genet, a condemnation was implicit in his birth, a birth which in fact (like all 'illegitimate' births) disrupted the order of the world, or, as Sartre says, moving from the empirical psychological to the ontological level, introduced a fissure in the plenitude of being.

Sartre goes on to show how Genet is 'faulty' not only from the

[1] *Saint Genet*, p. 15.

point of view of being, but also from that of having. He knew that he did not belong entirely to his adoptive parents, and could be reclaimed by the administration. Nothing could belong to him, material possession was forbidden him, all his life had to be a continued effort to dematerialize objects and construct their metaphysical doubles, which alone he could possess. The child Genet played two favourite solitary games, that of being a saint (to compensate for his insufficiency of being), and that of being a thief (to compensate for his inability to have). He was always alone, he had no experience of the omniscient, omnipotent mother who knows her child inside out, even to the extent of hearing his secret interior voice. No family ceremony occurred to consecrate the union of his identity for himself with his identity for others. Alone, without even an imaginary witness to his secrets, Genet lived in a state of concubinage with himself, he made a cult of himself, and resorted to archaic myths of the double. Genet then elected God to be the witness of his inner life. God filled the role of the absent mother. By becoming the object of the care of an infinite Being, Genet acquired a being for himself, he became a saint for want of being a son.

Genet's other game was to steal from his adoptive parents and their neighbours to achieve the imaginary experience of appropriation. The owner is one who has and uses his possessions without having to say 'Thank you'. Genet therefore took the possessions of others in secret to use them in solitude. Without inheritance or birthright, his earliest thefts were groping attempts to establish a relation of possession to things, a relation that was forbidden him otherwise, for everything he received from the Assistance Publique or from his adoptive parents was a gift for which he was indebted.

Genet resorted to this double compensatory activity because he could not destroy the very system of values which refused him his place in the world. His thefts and his dreams of saintliness were not opposed to the peasant morality, but in fact were consequences of it. Genet had been instructed in a morality designed to justify and sanctify the ownership of property, and it was this morality which condemned him.

For the child who tries to have or be by solitary actions, such stealthy activity does not yet fully exist unless seen by adults. To have and to be, Genet had to be seen and therefore condemned.

This, then, is the picture which Sartre paints of the boy Genet before his 'crisis'. God replaces his absent mother, and theft replaces property. His state of sweet confusion with nature would be interrupted in moments by a theft, or by an ecstasy, and this sufficed to maintain his internal equilibrium. But while he stole in innocence and dreamed of saintliness, Genet remained unaware that he was forging a destiny for himself.

Sartre's account of what he calls Genet's 'original crisis' assumes a central significance in the analysis. This original crisis was not a single isolated experience decisive for Genet's subsequent development, but was rather a prototypical mode of Genet's experience of himself-for-others at a stage of his childhood.

For Sartre it does not greatly matter whether the original crisis experience he describes was real or imaginary. Genet repeatedly refers to experiences of this sort—real or imaginary or both—as when he writes that the 'melodious child' was killed in him by 'a vertiginous word'. This murder may have taken place as the result of one verbal blow, or as the result of repeated 'traumata' of a similar kind.

The experience Sartre describes is as follows: one day, when ten years old, Genet was playing in the kitchen. Quite suddenly, in a spasm of anguish, he felt his aloneness, and plunged into an ecstatic state (*absenté*). His hand entered an open drawer. He became aware that someone had entered the room and was watching him. Under the look of this other person Genet 'came to himself' in a sense for the first time. Until that moment he had lacked an identity. Now he became confirmed. All at once he became a certain Jean Genet. He was blinded and deafened. He was an alarm bell which kept on ringing. Soon the whole village would know the answer to the question 'Who is Jean Genet?' Only the child

himself remained ignorant. Then a voice announced his identity
... 'You are a thief!'

His action, which for Genet had been nothing more than the
unreflective functioning of his subjectivity, became suddenly
transformed into the objective, and Genet experienced himself as
an object for the other. 'The thief' was a monstrous principle
which had been residing unperceived within him, and which was
now disclosed as his Truth, his eternal essence. Had he been six-
teen or seventeen, Genet might have rebelled against the judge-
ment and challenged the values of his elders, but he was a child, a
timid and respectful child who had been brought up religiously,
with a passionate love of goodness and saintliness. The 'honest
people' penetrated to the depths of his heart and left a permanent
residue of 'otherness', a part of Genet himself which was other
than himself. When he sought refuge from the condemnation of
other people by withdrawing into himself, he would meet within
himself an even worse condemnation. He became his own gaoler.
Even the most innocent-seeming desire he entertained became the
desire of a thief, and therefore guilt-ridden. It was through this
experience of accusation that Genet emerged from his state of
'sweet confusion with nature' and discovered that unknowingly
he had been becoming a person, and that this person was a
monster, and that whatever he might make of his life one thing
was henceforth forbidden him, namely to accept himself.

Sartre described how the 'good people' effected this metamorphosis of the child for social, utilitarian reasons, because of
their need for a scapegoat. For the good people, goodness is
equated with being, with that which already is, and evil with that
which calls being in question, with negation, non-being, otherness.
The argument cannot be reproduced here in detail, but essentially
it is this: the 'good man' perpetually denies the negative moment
of his actions. He affirms without denying the contrary of that
which he affirms. His permitted actions are to maintain, to conserve, to restore, to renew. These are the categories of repetition
as opposed to those of change. But the spirit, as Hegel says, is

unrest, and this unrest inspires the good man with horror. He then cuts off from his freedom its negative moment and projects it outside himself. In this the good man becomes himself the most abstract negation, the negation of his own negation.

The wicked man is an invention of the good man, the incarnation of his otherness to what he is, his own negative moment. All evil, for Sartre, is projection.[1] The honest people are able to hate in Genet that part of themselves which they have denied and projected into him. As an analogy, Sartre describes the industry which used to flourish in Bohemia in which such honest people took little children, split their lips, compressed their skulls, and imprisoned them day and night in boxes to prevent growth. They thus produced monsters which they were able profitably to exhibit. Similarly, but by more subtle means, people transformed Genet into a monster for reasons of social utility.

As a child Genet had no defences available against this technique practised against him by the adults who surrounded him. He affirmed the priority of the object which he was in their eyes over the subject which he was for himself. He became confused over the reality and the appearance of himself, and sacrificed his intimate feelings of intuitive certainty about himself to the principle of authority of the adults. His being an object for the others had priority over his being a subject for himself, and he experienced himself as being, in the depths of himself, a being other than himself. Sartre sets out to retrace the steps of Genet's self-alienation, the process by which he became a stranger to himself because of his progressive interiorization of the sentence passed on him by the adults.

Sartre examines the possibilities that appear to have presented themselves to Genet after his condemnation. First, what if he were to ask the honest people how he might make reparation for his badness? But the answer is only 'Be abject', and this is no solution for Genet, because he had already fallen into abjection and wished to escape from this way of being. This is only an apparent alterna-

[1] See *Saint Genet* pp. 33ff.

tive, for to choose this 'exit' from the untenable position which the honest people offer him can only mean that he enters further into their trap, that is, his *accepting* himself as what they have made of him.

Another exit might have been to become mad, but Genet is too straight, too real, too full of will (*trop 'volontaire'*) to resort to imaginary evasions. Here, however, Sartre appears to be guilty of a *petitio principii* in so far as Genet, as *trop volontaire*, too full of the capacity to choose, *could* hardly choose that mode of abdication of choice which is psychosis, as Sartre sees it. It is unfortunate that Sartre does not elaborate his meaning at this point in his argument.

Again, the way of suicide is barred by Genet's 'optimism', by which Sartre says he means 'the very orientation of his freedom' (*par là j'entends désigner l'orientation même de sa liberté*[1]). Sartre contrasts Genet with those in certain extreme situations who, when a certain limit of horror is passed, are aware only of the absurdity of the world, and relinquish their claim to life. Genet clutches desperately to his life in the unreasoning belief that he will 'come out on the other side', that his extreme situation will have some *issue*. In fact, since he did not choose suicide, it became *necessary* that his original situation have an issue, despite the evidence. Poetry was this issue.

It will not be possible within this chapter to consider the detailed working out of Genet's project to become a poet, but in the early situation of prototypical crisis Sartre finds the germinal structure of the poet. He writes admiringly of this child, who, at an age when most of us engage in servile efforts to please our parents, unflinchingly willed himself:

'Une volonté si farouche de survivre, un courage si pur, une confiance si folle au sein du désespoir porteront leur fruit: de cette resolution absurde naîtra vingt ans plus tard le poète Jean Genet'.[2]

[1] *Saint Genet*, p. 50.
[2] See *Saint Genet*, p. 55.

And later Genet writes of this early extreme choice of himself:
'J'ai décidé d'être ce que le crime a fait de moi.'

Since he could not escape fatality, he became his own fatality.
Since his life was rendered unlivable by the others, he would live
this impossibility of living as if he had created this destiny exclusively for himself. This is the destiny he willed—he would even
try to love this destiny.

Sartre is at pains to stress that Genet's 'original crisis' can be
understood only when seen against the setting of the French
village community, with its narrow and rigid system of prohi-
bitions, its high degree of cohesiveness, and the absolute value
given to private property. In this setting one can understand the
reaction of scandal and the diffusion of repressive sanctions against
the ten-year-old thief.

If he had been brought up in an industrial area, Genet would
have heard the very right to private possessions being contested,
and would have discovered that one *is* also what one *makes* and
does. Sartre gives a detailed analysis of the dialectical interaction
of the town and the country, and the 'society of producers' and
'society of consumers', and this analysis cannot be detached from
a consideration of Genet's concrete relations with others, and his
sexuality and creative work. However, since our study is centred
mainly on the latter areas, Sartre's original work should be
consulted for a detailed treatment of the former.

Having given an objective (*en soi*) account of Genet's early
decision to be that which his crime made him, Sartre goes on to
examine the decision as it was *for Genet* as the subjective moment
of his consciousness in its intentional structure. Here we encounter, Sartre says, an insurmountable contradiction. What can
I decide to be if I am already what I am: if I am 'locked up in my
being'? The word 'being' for Genet assumes an active, positive
value, and in the phrase 'J'ai décidé d'être ce que le crime a fait
de moi', to be is to throw oneself into one's being in order to
coincide with it.

The ambiguity of Genet's project is the ambiguity of our

condition. We are the beings whose being is perpetually in question: the meaning of our being is to be in question in our being. No man is cowardly or courageous as this wall is white or that book is black. For the coward, cowardice is manifested always as a possibility which can be refused or accepted, one can flee from it, undergo it without participating in it, one can find it even in actions which others judge to be brave.

Prior to his decision to be what his crime had made of him, namely a thief, Genet's being had not been in question for himself since he had been pure subject and pure object. This being which he believed himself to have received from the adults was that of being a person in one of the senses of the Latin *persona*—a mask or a role with pre-established patterns of conduct. It was a being in-itself and for-others, and not a being-for-itself. By his decision to be that which the others had made him be, Genet effected a forceful conjunction between pure willing (*pour-soi*, subjectivity), which defined him *après coup* by the totality of his acts, and a substance (*en-soi*, objectivity) which was prior to his acts and which appeared to produce these acts by a kind of internal necessity. Faced with a choice between existing a pure subjectivity or a pure objectivity—an apparently insoluble contradiction —Genet saved himself from madness and suicide by an heroic act of cheating. But he had still to find some place in the world, a sanctuary where the Other was not installed before him.

Sartre gives what he calls a static description of the incompatible systems of values which Genet uses simultaneously to think the world. According to Sartre, the special meanings conferred by Genet on each of these categories render them incompatible pairs.

I. *Categories of Being*	II. *Categories of Doing*
Object	Subject, consciousness
Himself as another	Himself
The essential which reveals itself inessential	Inessential which reveals itself essential
Fatedness	Liberty, will

Tragedy	Comedy
Death	Life, will to live
Hero	Saint
Criminal	Traitor
Loved one	Lover
Male principle	Female principle

As we shall see later, Genet has rendered the above categories of Being and Doing incompatible and then has conferred on them a false unity by a further sleight-of-hand. This double decision of Genet is highly dynamic. It transforms itself in contact with experience, it lives and enriches itself through the years. The dialectic of the perpetual interweaving of Genet's categories of being and doing renders unintelligible any attempt to study this pseudo-totality in terms of its own false syncretic togetherness. Sartre's method, therefore, is to proceed with partial analyses of the two sets of categories, and later, by a study of their reciprocal interaction, to reconstitute the concrete totality of Genet's private synthesis.

Sartre employs this analytic-synthetic method in relation to Genet's sexuality in this way.[1] Genet, Sartre writes, is a *raped child*. The first act of rape was the look of the other in his original crisis. This look surprised and *penetrated* him and transformed him into an object for ever. Sartre insists that he is not saying that Genet's original crisis was *like* a rape. It *was* rape.

The events we experience occur simultaneously on all levels of our life, and on each level are expressed in a different language. A physical violation can become a condemnation on the level of moral awareness, and, conversely, a condemnation can be experienced as a violation on the level of bodily awareness. In both cases the person is objectified, and if he experiences this objectification as shame in his heart, he experiences it in his body as a sexual act to which he has been subjected.

[1] Most of Sartre's ideas on Genet's sexuality are to be found in the chapter entitled 'The Eternal Couple of the Criminal and the Saint'.

Genet's back has become central in his sexual cult. When the child stole he was surprised *from behind*. In all subsequent acts of stealing his back stands out in his bodily awareness. It is with his back that he awaits the catastrophic look of the other. He experiences himself as objectified through his buttocks and back.

His penis is experienced not as a knife or sword but as a lifeless *thing* which only becomes rigid to give a better grip and to be handled more easily. It is typical of the homosexual experience of the penis, Sartre writes, that Proust did not call the penis a sword or scythe like the village lads, but a grappling-iron. Whereas the male experiences an erection as an aggressive stiffening of a muscle, for Genet it is more the blossoming of a flower. Whether the experienced erection is the swelling of a chamber with inert gas, or the unsheathing of a sword, nothing is decided in advance, for it is the total choice which a person makes of himself which gives its meaning to this intimate experience of the body. One man experiences his transcendence in his penis, another his passivity. It is true in fact that penile erection is a process of hardening (active), but it is also true that this hardening is something undergone (passive). The simple fact is ambiguous.

The priority in the subject himself of the object over the subject[1] leads to passivity in love, and in the male to homosexuality. Genet, having found that he could not realize his being without the mediation of others, went on to make his objectivity for others the essential and his reality for himself the inessential. His wish was to be handled passively by the other in order to become an object for his own eyes. The situation of any man who finds his truth in his being-for-the-other Sartre calls pre-pederastic. There is something of this in actors, even when they have a sexual preference exclusively for women.

The male does not usually wish to seduce a woman by his

---

[1] Sartre has been criticized on the ground of his maintaining a false subject-object dualism, but it should be noted here that he is making a phenomenological study of a person, and the experiences of oneself as a subject-for-oneself and as an object-for-others clearly need linguistic differentiation to express the phenomenological contrast in modes of self-experience.

physical attributes, which he has received and not achieved. The woman must love him for his potency, his courage and aggressiveness, as a force without features, as a pure power of doing and taking. Such a man seeks a reflection of his infinite liberty in the eyes of the submitting woman. But Genet who *does* nothing, who acts only in order to be, seeks to reveal to the other not his force, but his essence. His acts have efficacy only in appearance—they are *gestures*.

In his novel *Notre Dame des Fleurs* his principal character is a male prostitute who is so feminized that he feels himself to be a woman and is called Divine. Genet describes him throughout as 'her'. At one point 'she' seeks to become a man by attempting male actions—but they remain only gestures. She whistles and puts her hands in her pockets, but this performance is so badly executed that in the course of an evening she appears as five or six different male characters at once. She shows herself off, makes herself an object; she wishes to be taken and not to take, to be seen but not to look at.

One is not born a homosexual, Sartre argues, but one may become one according to the accidents of one's history and one's reaction to these accidents. Everything depends on what one does to what is done to one. Homosexuality, in this view, is the result not of some pre-natal determination, nor of an endocrine malfunction, neither is it the passive and determined result of complexes. It is an outcome discovered or invented by a child at a critical moment, a moment of suffocation.

Other factors also led Genet to homosexuality. He reacted to his condemnation by a radical ethical inversion. As he says, he was turned inside out like a glove, he was the monster, the unnatural, the impossible. Not only was he excluded from the natural world, but he was excluded from his own nature.

'We bathe in our life, in our blood and sperm: our body is a thick fluid stream which carries us along, and it is enough that we allow this to happen. A commonplace Venus, hardly distinguishing the alimentary and respiratory movements and the beating of the heart, gently leads us to a woman. It is enough for us to have confidence in this servant goddess and to leave it all to her'.[1]

But Genet is dead, his life is no more natural than his birth. This life haunts a corpse: Genet clings on to life only by his will. If he becomes aware of the suffocated sensations which arise in his bodily organs, he experiences himself as impossible and falls into a state of wonder. He finds in himself none of the powerful instincts which sustain the desires of the honest man; he knows only the instinct of death. His sexual desires, like his life itself, will be phantoms. Whatever their object, they are condemned in advance: for him there is an original prohibition against desire. His inverted sexuality, his singular rejection of the rules of the others, the principle of *contra-nature*, antiphysis, are reflected in the plan of his body as he experiences it.

It remains to be seen how Genet chose between a male and a female homosexual role. For him the male partner is the loved one. By playing this role the male rediscovers himself magnified in the heart of the lover (the female partner). He is saved and in a place of shelter. Genet however chose the female role, the consequences of which are the pain of bearing the indifference of the other, jealousy, and finally despair in the certitude of the loved one's indifference, of being unloved. But in the magical ceremony of intercourse the lover steals the being of the loved one to incorporate it. Genet's writings abound with images representing this theme, and he is highly conscious of his use of this fantastic interchange of identities.[2]

The earliest form of love which Genet remembers was a wish *to be* a good-looking boy he saw pass by, and not *to have* the boy

[1] *Saint Genet*, p. 83.

[2] cf. the psycho-analyst's discerning in unconscious phantasy "mechanisms" of projective and introjective identification.

For a fuller treatment of this subject from a phenomenological and existential analytic point of view the reader is referred to *The Self and Others* by R. D. Laing (1961).

sexually. Divine says to Gabriel, 'You are myself', and Gabriel smiles fatuously, unaware that the other is sucking his blood in an act of magical vampirism. The passionate love which the lieutenant has for Querelle is the desire to tear off Querelle's genitals and graft them on to himself.

To some, these projects of projective and introjective identification may appear absurd, but, Sartre says, how sure are such people of being themselves. He relates how, when once he heard a man start announcing 'We doctors . . .', he knew this man to be a slave. This 'We doctors . . . ' was his self as co-extensive with his internalized others, the parasitic creatures who sucked his blood. 'It is permitted to no-one to say these simple words: I am myself.'[1] Only the most free can say 'I exist'—and that is already too much. Most people should use formulas such as 'I am himself', 'I am such a one in person'. This socially accepted alienation Sartre calls 'a legitimate hell', and he expresses his distaste for these 'inhabited souls'. He writes:

'If for yourself you are already another, if you suffer from a perpetual absence in your heart, then you may live this absence as if it were that of no matter which other: this other will never be more absent than you are, for the manner in which he is not himself (that is to say, in which he himself is another for himself), the manner in which you are not yourself and that in which you are not he do not differ sensibly.'[2]

Sartre compares Genet to an empty palace. The tables are all laid, the candles are lit, footsteps resound in the corridors, doors open and shut, but nobody appears. He has lain in wait, and set traps and installed mirrors, but all in vain.

To be loved was Genet's impossible dream. The honest people, we have seen, projected into Genet their negative powers and made him incarnate these. Genet then projects this absolute otherness into the loved one. As a stranger to himself he can love

[1] *Saint Genet*, p. 85.
[2] Ibid, p. 85.

only another who is other-than-himself. He is loved only by himself, for it is himself in his absolute otherness that loves him in the guise of the other. It is not simply the muscles, the hair, and the smell of the other which penetrate him, but all these things as the incarnation of being, *his* being. In loving this indifferent beauty with all his body and spirit, Genet, the abandoned child, achieves his supreme end of *being loved*—but loved not as himself by another, but by himself in his otherness in another.

The essence of the loved one is his *indifference*, his profound nature of being a thing, an object. Genet conceives of the couple as the union of body and spirit, but this relation is not reciprocal, since consciousness may be consciousness of body, but body is quite simply body, body is completely itself. The body in itself (*en soi*) is an autonomous substance; consciousness is in itself and for itself a relation. It is this autonomy of substance that Genet calls indifference. All the words he uses to designate the loved one are negations or disguised negations—for example, 'immobile and silent', 'inflexible', 'impenetrable', 'the angel of death itself, as unyielding as a rock'. The loved one is absent, or present only as an appearance. His purest virtues are his destructive forces and his lack of positive qualities. In the moment of submission Genet reduces the male to a shadow, an appearance of being which exists only through Genet. This is the principal source of Genet's *treachery*.

The loved male is above all the No: non-life, non-love, non-presence, non-good. Destiny for Genet is a giant penis, man is completely phallus, the phallus becomes man. Sartre notes many of Genet's images which illustrate his 'pan-sexualism', and his phallicization of nature. But this pan-sexualism is a pan-moralism and this sexualized universe lacks sensuality. This penis is metallic: that of Paulo, for instance, is described as a cannon. Genet is not disturbed by the flesh of a penis, but by its power of penetration and its mineral hardness. Sartre refers to Bachelard's Icarus complex and shows how Genet's sexuality involves the dynamics of *the Fall*. Genet falls into the heart of the other and as he falls a vertiginous phallic cliff stretches up higher and higher, the deeper the abyss into which he falls. Finally at the bottom of the abyss the lover, Genet, finds the corpse of the loved one who has fallen before him.

The sexual act for Genet is a ceremony of submission. But the act is also always an act of rape, for, in submitting, his pride puts up a considerable resistance which finds a bodily representative in the resistance of his anal sphincter.

The sexual act is a repetition of the crisis which transformed Genet into a thief. In both he is nailed down by the look of cruel, strong men. But in this case the crisis is sought after and provoked and, in Sartre's view, has a kathartic value similar to that of the psycho-analytic process.

In this austere ceremony there is little sensuality. The male partner never caresses the other, unless it be roughly to shift his position to facilitate his own pleasure. Orgasm is refused to the lover during coitus, during which it is both true and false that Genet experiences pleasure. There is pleasure 'in him', but it is the other who takes this pleasure. After coitus Divine rapidly and discreetly masturbates in the lavatory behind the back of Notre-Dame, her male partner.

There are two phases in Genet's sexual act—the 'strong' phase in which the other is present, but pleasure absent and the 'weak' phase where pleasure is really present but the other absent. When the other is really present pleasure is imaginary and merely simulated. In the 'weak' phase of masturbation pleasure is really present but it is accompanied only by phantasms—Divine thinks of Notre-Dame while he masturbates, although Notre Dame, asleep and snoring, has forgotten him.

Sartre develops his account of the function of masturbation in Genet's life in the following passage:

'All the prisoners indulge in masturbation, but usually it is for want of something better. They would prefer the most decrepit prostitute to this solitary luxury. In short, they make "good use" of the Imaginary. They are the honest onanists. A French journalist in Cincinnati, disgusted by American puritanism, once nobly announced: "I, a man of thirty-five years with a croix-de-guerre and four children, I masturbated this morning!" There is an honest man. But Genet would make a "bad use" of masturbation. To decide to prefer appearances above all is on principle to place masturbation higher than all forms of coition.'

Genet's tough young 'loved ones' are entirely dependent on him for their existence as such: why should he not altogether eliminate the 'real' other?

'*Images* would amply suffice to manifest the great homosexual essences. This phrase of Genet's seems to me admirably to define his masturbation: "I exist only through those who do not exist but for the being they receive from me."

'An onanist by choice, Genet prefers his own caresses because the enjoyment received coincides with the enjoyment given, the passive moment coincides with the moment of greatest activity: he is at the same time this consciousness which coagulates and this hand which becomes agitated and churns. Being, existence; faith, works; masochistic inertia and sadistic ferocity; petrification and freedom: in the moment of pleasure the two contradictory components of Genet coincide, he is the criminal who rapes and the saint who allows herself to be raped. On his body a hand caresses Divine. Or, better, the hand which caresses him is the hand of Mignon. The onanist derealizes himself, he is close to discovering the magical formulas which will open the sluice-gates. Genet has disappeared: Mignon makes love with Divine. However, victim or executioner, caresser or the one caressed, these spectres must finally be reabsorbed into Narcissus: Narcissus fears men, fears their judgements and their real presence: he wishes only to experience for himself an aura of love, only to distance himself slightly from his body, only for a thin layer of otherness to coat his flesh and his thoughts. His characters melt; this lack of consistency reassures him and serves his sacrilegious designs; it caricatures love. The masturbator bewitches himself as he can never sufficiently feel himself to be another, and himself produces the diabolic appearance of a couple which fades away when touched. The failure of pleasure is the acid pleasure in failure. A pure demonic act, masturbation sustains in the heart of consciousness an appearance of appearance: masturbation is the derealization of the world and of the masturbator himself. But this man who arranges to be eaten up by his own dream realizes only too well that his dream exists only because of his willing it; Divine does not stop absorbing Genet into her, nor Genet reabsorbing Divine into him. However, by a reversal which brings ecstasy to the point of overflowing, this lucid negation provokes real events in the world: the erection, ejaculation, the damp stains on the bed covers are caused by the imaginary. In a single movement the masturbator captures the world in order to dissolve it and to insert the order of the unreal into the universe: the images must *exist* since they act. No, the masturbation of Narcissus is not, as people vainly think, a trivial gallantry which is performed in the evenings, a mischievous but nice compensation for the day's labours; it wills itself to be a crime. Genet has extracted his pleasure from his nothingness: solitude, impotence, the unreal, evil have produced, without recourse to being, an *event* in the world.'[1]

We see here in Genet's use of masturbation an expression of his way of resolving into a false unity the contradictions he himself invents. This project lies at the base of all Genet's thought and actions. All the early attributions made about Genet's nature to the effect that his nature was unnatural (antiphysis) concealed an injunction which he experienced as a prohibition against having any 'natural', spontaneous thought or feeling. Every spontaneous desire which is immediately aimed at its own gratification encounters a reflective consciousness which forbids its gratification.

[1] *Saint Genet*, p. 341-2.

Every feeling, every form of primary awareness, is accompanied by a parasitic reflective awareness which directs, contradicts, or manipulates the primary awareness. This condition is probably general in sophisticated people to some extent, but with Genet it is the rule.

'The ambiguous structures, these false unities where the two terms of a contradiction chase after each other in an infernal rondo, these I call tourniquets'.[1]

Although Genet is tortured by his reflective consciousness, it is also true that his optimism and his lucidity reside in it. His spontaneous primary awareness becomes faded and less vital, ultimately nothing more than a transparent, gelatinous membrane between the world and his reflective consciousness. Genet sees the world through the medium of his primary awareness rather than by it. A pane of glass rather than an eye, it serves to diminish the threatening aspect of the world. He is an audience sitting in at the drama of his own misfortunes. His, Sartre writes, is a consciousness stuffed full with itself, like the prunes of Tours.

This mode of operation of his consciousness is experienced by Genet in a stupor of perplexity. Sometimes he would ask himself if he were dreaming, and reality would have the aftertaste of a nightmare. But his stupor above all is reflective. Sartre asks us to imagine the strange taste which this consciousness has of itself. 'Who am I?' 'Why am I alone to suffer so much?' 'What have I done to be here?' 'Who puts me to these trials?' To all these questions there is only one reply: Genet himself is the reply. He finds the answer in finding himself. At each moment there is a promise to be kept, at each moment he grasps hold of himself as a vocation. But who is it who calls? What promise has he made? To whom? At times he would fall into a state of wonder so profound that he felt himself to be losing consciousness. At the reformatory at Mettray in the dining-room he would sit with his

[1] Ibid. p. 238. *Tourniquet* has been translated 'whirligig' by Bernard Frechtman, but I shall use the French term here in the hope that it will acquire its correct, specific connotation from the context.

fork poised in the air, his eyes staring vaguely, forgetting to eat. The authorities had him examined by a psychiatrist, but, Sartre says, these 'stupors' were a proof of his sanity. Unlike those contemporary philosophers, such as Camus, who believe they have discovered the absurdity of the world and of man in the world, Genet finds the world to be too full of meaning. For Camus the thin crust of meanings sometimes melts to reveal a brute reality without significance. For Genet it is reality which is eroded away by a surfeit of strange meanings. In his 'stupor' Genet, in amazement, comprehends simultaneously reality and the results of his own acts of derealization. The stupor is a mode of 'contact with' and comprehension of reality, but reality comprehended in the mode of his estrangement from it.

Sartre gives many examples of Genetian *tourniquets*, the reflective techniques by which Genet deals with the paradoxes of his existence. He presents a set of general principles or schemata on which the construction of the *tourniquets* is based. Genet has developed a type of anti-logic, a *logique du faux*. A rapid oscillation from one position to its contradiction produces a semblance of identity, a false unity, which may immediately be followed by a further contradiction, which is similarly dealt with. The false unity, since it is impossible, is given only as a limit, as a term of a movement, a movement which cannot be a progression, since progress entails a synthesis of antithetical terms. The movement of Genet's thoughts is circular. Sartre compares Genet's disordering of reason with Rimbaud's systematic disordering of the senses. Recalling the two irreconcilably opposed systems of categories of Being and Doing one finds intricate dialectics operating within each system and between them.

If Genet asserts the proposition 'I am the weakest man of all and the strongest', what is he in fact saying? Is it that he is weak from some points of view and strong from certain others, or that he is weak 'in appearance' and strong 'in reality?' But Genet makes no such distinctions. He is both strong and weak at all moments and from all points of view, in appearance and in reality. He refers himself here to two opposed systems of value and refuses to choose either. In the first system, the 'active homosexual pimp' is Destiny, the marvellous appearance of pure evil, and Genet is nothing but the meanest crawling vermin, enslaved by his strict master. In the second system, Genet with his lucid awareness imprisons the pimp with his words and his charms, and leads him to disaster with his perfumed treachery. But each system implies the other. If the pimp is only a puppet whose strings are pulled by Genet, how does he find pleasure in the process? He must somehow retain his superiority over Genet, so that the latter, in fooling him, acquires his good qualities. Conversely, Genet the saint, when the pimp kicks him about, must retain his sense of superiority, so that evil may be perfect and injustice complete. He is strongest when he is the weakest and weakest when he is the most strong. If one operates here in terms of sado-masochism, one finds not composite or alternating states of sadistic or masochistic pleasure, but a sadism which has a secret dimension of masochism, and conversely.

It is not possible to communicate in an abridged form Sartre's exhaustive phenomenological analysis of the function of natural objects, tools and gadgets, and language in Genet's world. Genet's relation to objects is well shown in his experience of a burglary. Genet learns the density of being by the effort required to destroy it. Theft is a sacred act of destruction. In a burglary he must lift barriers, unhinge doors, kill any dogs, put alarms out of action. If all goes well he then *enters a man*, a naked, paralysed, defenceless man. The room reflects this man's tastes, habits, and vices.

'I do not exactly reflect on the owner of the place, but all my gestures evoke him. . . . I bathe in the idea of property when I rob the property. I recreate the absent owner. He exists not face to face with me but all around me. He is a fluid element which I breathe, which enters into me, which swells my lungs.'[1]

[1] *Saint Genet* p. 244. Genet quoted by Sartre.

But not only is this presence violated, it is mutilated. Gloved hands grope around inside the open belly. They tear out the liver and grab a family photograph album. This rape followed by murder is symbolic, and the thieves are so aware of this that they try to achieve a bodily realization of it. Certain thieves of whom Genet writes sit down and eat in the kitchen of the house they are robbing, or they defaecate or vomit over the money they take from a drawer. After this destruction another destructive act follows in the conversion of the value of an object from a use value to a value of exchange. Theft results, thus, in the radical destruction of the stolen object, the disorganization of the values of usefulness and sentimental association, an impoverishment of the world. Our acts sketch our form on being, the created object presents its creator to himself in an objective dimension. In creation I am really exteriorized amongst beings in the world: in destruction the universe is reabsorbed into me.

The material presented by Sartre falls readily into place in a psycho-analytic conceptual framework within which mechanisms such as introjective and projective identification, idealization of the object, denial and splitting operate. These mechanisms function in that realm of experience known as unconscious phantasy, and have their origin in early infantile life, to which, in the case of Genet, Sartre too often accords only an implicit and unsystematic recognition. One might say, for example, that in addition to feelings of rejection by his mother Genet had phantasies of having destroyed his mother in hatred, and that guilt over his sadistic attacks on his mother lies behind his experience of being caught and named a thief, and that this phantastic guilt gives a further, necessary meaning to the 'monstrous principle' in Genet, which was later 'projected into him' by the adults of his childhood world. To steal 'in reality' may be seen as coinciding with phantasies of stealing and spoiling the good contents of his mother's breast and her body, and Genet's experience of being named a thief may be seen against a background of 'unconscious guilt' related to these phantasy activities.

Genet might have lived the rest of his life like most of us, with his phantasies buried 'inside' him, although perhaps manifesting themselves indirectly as 'symptoms', and inaccessible to his reflective consciousness, had he not been placed in a position where the others attempted to establish their presence in him and henceforth to control him 'from the inside', in a manner which constituted a total threat to his identity, a threat of total alienation which would have left nothing of him for himself. They acted out his most terrible phantasies of the other, and this situation first brought his phantasies from the level of pre-reflective awareness, which is unconscious phantasy in so far as this is experience, to the level of imagination, which entails a reflective awareness. This transformation of phantasy (pre-reflective) into imaginative (reflective) awareness is the central issue. Genet's phantasies became the images of his myths. He might have become a psychotic 'victim' of his phantasies, but instead he mastered the phantasies through the imagination of his rituals and his writing.

It is possible to regard early phantasies as part of one's 'facticity'[1] —in the same way as a diseased body might be part of one's facticity. To what extent is one free to choose oneself, in the face of phantasies which seem to determine one's perception of oneself and of others, and which originate in a phase that is ontogenetically prior to responsibility in the ordinary sense of the term? And, as we have already noted (p. 74) on a cognate issue, the notion of Genet being *trop volontaire* gives rise to difficulties at this level of theoretical consideration. The very capacity to choose oneself may be seen as a genetically determined original 'constitutional' datum, but, as Sartre puts it, the facticity of freedom is that freedom is not free not to be free. Some of these matters are further elucidated in the *Critique of Dialectical Reason*.

---

[1] *Facticity*. This term, first used by Sartre in *Being and Nothingness*, refers to the manner in which a consciousness is necessarily embedded in the world, in materiality, and in the past of a person.

3. CRITIQUE OF DIALECTICAL REASON

3. CRITIQUE OF DIALECTICAL REASON

Introduction

A. DOGMATIC DIALECTIC AND CRITICAL DIALECTIC

There are certain basic principles of dialectical materialism, for example, that a negation of a negation can be an affirmation, that it is in and through conflict inside a person or a group that the person or the group makes history, that each moment of a series must be understood starting from the initial moment, *and is irreducible to it*, that history operates at each instant by totalizations of totalizations, and so on. But these are principles not dogmas. Some of these dialectical principles are found in other approaches. For instance, the determinism of the Comtian positivists is necessarily a materialism, but the object as studied by them is always a mechanism, in that it is conditioned from outside itself. Social anthropologists always use dialectical procedures to some extent, and psycho-analytic theory contains dialectical elements, but every existing theoretical system is in a hopelessly confused state as regards its basic principles.

Now, Sartre says that while he wishes to avoid dogma, there is such a thing as a hyperempiricism, a neo-positivism that rejects everything *a priori*. There is no reason why research should not be informed by principles. What must be remembered is that there is purely rational justification *neither* for exclusive recourse to analytical reason, *nor* for the unconditioned choice of dialectical reason. We must take the object as it is given and allow its free development to unfold before us.

The object of this study is the human scene in its full concrete reality. The present problem is: how can we think about the human scene so that it is intelligible, and in what way are we thinking if or when we do find it intelligible?

The greatest attempt to come to terms with this task is represented in the Marxist tradition, but at present there is a crisis in Marxist culture. Marxist theory has become temporarily arrested by inner contradictions that are at present not being resolved, but are being denied. The result is theoretical paralysis. Diogenes proved movement simply by walking, but what if he had been momentarily paralysed?

Research in the natural sciences does not necessarily need to be aware of its own basic principles in order to be operationally effective. Dialectical knowledge of objects, on the contrary, is inextricable from knowledge of the dialectic. The dialectic is a method of knowing, and a movement in the object known. The structure of the real and that of our own praxis are interlinked. Dialectical reason does not take a stance outside the system to which it must apply itself: it does not proceed by an initial working hypothesis, formulated outside the system to be investigated, and then applied to it. It *depasses*,[1] that is, it dissolves in itself without eliminating, the analytical reason of the seventeenth century as one moment in a larger synthesis.

The first task for a critique of dialectical reason is to ask what are its limits and what is its validity. Dialectical reason can be, indeed requires to be, criticized, in Kant's sense of the term, by dialectical reasoning itself. While this is true, it is necessary to allow this critique to find its own basis and development. This has not been done up to the present because such a critique has been blocked by dogmatism.

This dogmatism has persisted from the beginning—ever since Marx turned Hegel upside down. There is a sense in which Hegel's dogmatism is superior to a Marxist dogmatism, and this superiority lies *precisely in its idealism*. For in this very idealism a separation *and* a link existed between knowing and its object. It

[1] See p. 13 above.

94

is this separation which gets lost in Marx. Marx says that the material existence of men cannot be reduced to contemplative knowledge. Praxis swamps mere knowing. But we are immediately in difficulties. Thought is at one and the same time being and knowledge of being. It is the praxis of an individual or of a group in determined conditions at a particular moment of history. As such, thought is subject to dialectics as its law, in the same way as any detail of historical processes. But thought as reason is also knowledge of the dialectic. That is, from this latter point of view it is the very law to which it is subject. Is there an irresolvable contradiction between knowledge of being and the being of knowledge? In so far as it is *constitutive of being*,[1] thought manifests a dialectic of activity and passivity. It is simultaneously constitutive and constituted.

Hegel tries to resolve this problem by postulating the ultimate identity of being and knowledge. Marx is also monistic. But the monism either of Hegel or of Marx is split by its contradictions into a dualism. Marx has defined his ontological monism by his thesis that being cannot be reduced to thought. On the contrary, he seeks to absorb his thoughts into being. But this monistic affirmation is given as a dogmatic truth. In Sartre's view, dialectical materialism is superior to contemporary ideologies in practice, since it is the ideology of the rising class, and so is necessarily occupied with demystifying and clarifying itself. But this would be simply the expression of an unintelligible thing-like inert process, and not a praxis, if it could not turn round on itself to clarify itself: it would be no better than the methods that make up philosophical liberalism. Monistic materialism has very happily suppressed the old dualism of thought and being in order to grasp being as a whole in its materiality. But in so doing, monistic materialism denies any dialectical relationship between

---

[1] Constitutive—constituted: cf. Kant's constitutive principles of reason as opposed to regulative principles. The former enable us to extend our concept of the sensible world beyond all possible experience, e.g. mathematics; the latter postulate operations to be performed without anticipating what is present in the object 'as it is in itself'. Sartre develops constituting and constituted as antithetic active/passive terms in a dialectic.

thought and being. Contemporary Marxists seem to be paralysed by this difficulty. If thought is only part of the historical process, seen as a sort of mechanically developing thing, then no ideology can be more true than the next. Monistic Marxism, but *not* a truly conceived dialectic, falls into total relativism. Modern monistic Marxism, however, in refusing in effect a dialectical activity to thought, and in attempting to dissolve thought into a cosmic dialectic, suppresses man. It kneads, dissolves, disintegrates him into the universe. After this has been done, there is then properly speaking nothing to which being can be said to manifest itself. The Marxist dialectic of nature invents a nature without man.

Knowledge, on the contrary, whatever form it takes, is a certain relationship of man with the world. If man does not exist any more this relationship disappears. Whitehead said very accurately that a law of nature begins as an hypothesis and ends by becoming a 'fact'. When we say that the earth revolves, we do not have the feeling of putting forward a proposition, or of referring ourselves to a system of knowledge. We think that we are in the presence of the 'fact' itself, so much so that suddenly we eliminate ourselves as the knowing subjects, and by a further disappearing trick eliminate our act of self-elimination. Knower and knowledge suppress themselves to become each simply in the world as parts of it. Now, this is true, not only of philosophers and philosophy, but of scientists and scientific knowledge. When dialectical materialism pretends to establish a dialectic of nature, it does not reveal itself as an attempt to establish a general synthesis of human knowledge, but as a simple organization of 'facts'. It would be quite wrong to pretend to be occupied with 'facts' when the 'facts' themselves risk being modified in their very essence by the progress of science. This attempt to speak of the world as though it revealed itself to no one can be called transcendental dialectical materialism.

This form of materialism is not really dialectical, and yet it is in Marx that we find its definition: 'a materialistic concept of the world signifies merely the conception of the world as it is without any extraneous addition from outside.' In this conception, man is put into the heart of nature as one of its objects, and is supposed to have developed under our eyes in compliance with the laws of nature: that is to say, as pure materiality governed by the supposedly universal laws of the dialectic. In this view, the object of thought is taken to be nature as such itself. The study of history is seen simply as one instance of the study of nature. This conception has the advantage of conjuring away the problem. In it the dialectic of nature is transcendental and *a priori*, and the nature of man resides outside himself in a nature which is extra-human, in a history which begins with the nebulae. Everything must go back all the time to the totality of natural history, of which human history is one instance. Within this theoretical scheme, real thought as praxis cannot be conceived. Dialectically grasped, real thought transcends prior moments within the concrete movement of history, but in this non-dialectical materialism thought can hardly be more than an imperfect reflection of its objects, which at best it will distort as little as possible. An idea is true only in so far as one can reduce it to a dead object, to a resultant. True thought would be the least human, the least alive, *the perfect resultant. The idea becomes a thing, signified by things, and not a signifying act.* The concrete, living man, with his human relationships, his thoughts, true and false, his actions, his real objectives, is a foreign body to this system, which has closed, leaving him outside. In his place is an absolute object, for to the dogmatic Marxist what is called a subject is nothing more than an object considered as the centre of particular reactions. Yet, at the moment of success of this sceptical objectivism, we wake up to discover that it has been imposed on us by an attitude of dogmatism, or, in other terms, that this objectivism is the truth of being making its supposed appearance to a universal consciousness; some sort of universal mind presumably *sees* the dialectic as the law of the world. The result of all this is that we have fallen into complete dogmatic idealism.

Natural-scientific laws are derived from experimental hypotheses that have been verified by facts. The absolute principle that 'nature is dialectical' is, on the contrary, incapable of any verification. As we have seen, there is clearly a dialectic *between* the scientist and his objects, but, if we declare that there is a dialectical movement *in* the objects of the laws established by science without further reference to the scientist, there is no way of proving this.

Dialectical reason has nothing to do with forces presumed to operate in the realm of physics and chemistry. The idea of dialectics has arisen in history in quite a different way, and has been discovered and defined in and through the relations of man to matter, and of man to man.

One has to watch here the ambiguity of language, which signifies sometimes objects and sometimes their concepts. Materialism is not in itself opposed to idealism. There is a materialistic idealism which is at heart only a discourse on the idea of matter. The true opposite of idealistic materialism is realistic materialism. Thought is the thought of a man. It begins from the fact that he is situated in the world, implicated by all the forces of the cosmos. It speaks of the material universe as that which is revealed out of a praxis in a particular situation.

Marxist doctrinaires feel they have achieved a real grasp of necessity, whereas what they have in fact done has been to precipitate their thoughts through a circuit of alienation, in that they have converted their own lived thinking into an object for a universal consciousness and have then re-appropriated this universal consciousness as if it belonged to them.

Engels reproaches Hegel for imposing on matter the laws of thought, but this is what Engels does himself. Natural science is an enterprise of natural scientists, and as such it is an historical and social enterprise. *History and the Social are the only true realms of dialectical reason.* To transport the dialectic into the natural world from which the scientist has been plucked is to deprive it of rationality, because it is then no longer a dialectic that man makes in making himself.

This does not mean that Sartre denies the existence of dialecti-

CRITIQUE OF DIALECTICAL REASON

cal relationships in inanimate nature. His position is that one can believe or not believe that the laws of physics and chemistry manifest a dialectic. But here it is a question of reason in a regulative sense, not in a constitutive sense. It is necessary to establish the limits and the validity of dialectical evidence. A dialectic of nature is possible but not necessary. Only through the interior of human history, that is, through the praxis of men located within concrete material conditions, that is, through the discovery of those conditions and of man's subjection to them, does a dialectic manifest itself. In a word, if there exists something which one can properly call dialectical materialism, this must be an historical materialism, that is to say, a materialism from within history. I, you, he, she, make, undergo, live, know it. By the same token, this materialism, if it exists, can obtain only within the limits of our social universe, at the heart of our organized, stratified society. In contrast, the dialectic of nature can only be a metaphysical hypothesis. The mental procedure which consists in (a) discovering in and through praxis the dialectical rationality of our actions in their historical and social context, (b) projecting this rationality as an unconditioned law into the inorganic world, and then (c) bringing it back from the inorganic into society under the pretence that this law of nature in its opaque irrationality conditions society, is about as perverse and devious as can be imagined. One meets a human relationship, which one grasps because one is oneself a man, one turns it into a thing, one strips it of all human character, and, finally, one substitutes this thing, quite irrational and contrived, for the true relationship which one has met in the first place. In the name of monism one replaces the practical rationality of man making history by the blindness of natural necessity. One substitutes the obscure for the clear, the conjectural for the evident, science-fiction for truth.

If there is a true dialectic, we know where to look for its basis. We will accept the idea that man is a material being among others, and that he does not enjoy as such any privileged status. We will not refuse *a priori* the possibility that a concrete dialectic of nature can one day be revealed. The dialectical method may be of interpretative value in the sciences of nature, and be utilized by scientists themselves under the control of experience. But dialectical reason must be grasped where it gives itself for us to see, in place of dreaming it up. And it is seen in the material conditions of history. But if one means by dialectical or historical materialism a monism which is taken to govern human history *from outside*, irrespective of the actions of men, then it is necessary to say that this does not exist.

Engels's error was to suppose that he could derive dialectical laws of nature from procedures which were themselves non-dialectical: comparisons, analogies, abstractions, inductions. In fact, dialectical reason is a whole, and must find its basis in itself. That is to say, by a dialectical method.

In the polarity of being and knowing, neither can be reduced to the other. But we must be careful that this dualism does not lead to some disguised idealism. The only possibility that a dialectic exists is itself dialectical, or, if one prefers, the only possible unity of dialectic, as law of historical development, and of dialectic, as knowledge in movement of this development, must be in the unity of a dialectical movement. Being is negation of knowing, and knowing draws its being from the negation of being.

'*Men make history*, on the basis of anterior conditions.' The universe evaporates in a dream if man is purely subject to the dialectic coming to him from the outside as his unconditioned law. In one *moment* (in the Hegelian sense) man is subject to the dialectic as an enemy power. In another moment he creates it. This second moment is the negation of the first, which is the negation of man. This is the crucial negation of negation. It is necessary, we are condemned, to live this contradiction dialectically. Man undergoes the dialectic, in so far as he makes it, and makes it, in so far as he undergoes it. He is not subject to it non-dialectically, like a divine law, or a metaphysical fatality: and it does not emanate from himself non-dialectically, as though he were its unconditioned creator.

The dialectic is the law of *totalization*. Collectives, societies, history, are realities that are imposed, or impose themselves, on individuals. Yet these realities are woven out of millions of individual actions. The thought that totalizes history is the resultant of history, but it is neither merely its passive vehicle, nor a transcendental fatality. It alone can realize each instant, and unify in its praxis the pulls towards dispersion and integration. Thus, in a *materialist* dialectic, as in the Hegelian, thought must discover both its own necessity and the necessity of its object.

There is no dialectic imposed on facts as the Kantian categories impose themselves on reality. The dialectic, if it exists, is the singular adventure of each person's relations with the objects of his experience. There are no categories, in anyone's head or in the sky: there is no pre-established scheme which can be imposed on these singular developments: the *dialectic* does not impose on historical man terrible contradictions in terms of which he has to live: but under the sway of scarcity and necessity the actions of men are such that dialectical rationality alone makes them intelligible. The dialectic, if it exists, can be only totalization of concrete totalizations carried out by a multiplicity of totalizing singularities.

To the necessity and the intelligibility of dialectical reason is joined the obligation to discover it empirically in each case, and this can be achieved only dialectically. Nothing can become dialectic seen from the point of view of analytic reason, that is, exterior to the object considered (e.g. the passivity of the scientist to a system, and the passivity of the system to him). The dialectic is revealed only to an observer situated inside the system. The dialectic is the living logic of action. It will be for us to show that it is universally and necessarily present as a possibility, as the adventure of all. It can be nothing other than its own total translucency. It is the rationality of praxis, of totalization, of social future.

That is, the experience of the dialectic is itself the dialectic praxis by which it is made.

The real end of this study is theoretical; one can formulate it in these terms: what are the conditions of the possibility of the knowledge of history in general, or of a region of history? What are the limits of the necessity of the relationships that are in play? What are the limits and the foundations of dialectical rationality?

B. CRITIQUE OF CRITICAL EXPERIENCE

While one can state the abstract conditions wherein dialectical experience is possible, this still leaves its singular reality undetermined. By what specific set of operations do we hope to manifest and prove the reality of the dialectical process? What is its point of application? What experimental system should we construct? Upon what facts do we base ourselves? Which experiences are critical?

Now, at present, we are concerned with articulating a scheme that will make intelligible the complex play of praxis and totalization. The problem is to give a critique of the instruments of thought whereby history is conceptualized intelligibly. If such a critique is itself a valid undertaking, what will be the criterion of the validity of our procedure?

Analytic-positive reason cannot make the dialectic intelligible, but analytic-positive reason can be understood in terms of dialectical reason. The validity of dialectical reason rests on its own translucency. It cannot be validated by any other form of reason, for the 'principles' of dialectical reason do not fall within the framework of any other form of reason—they are not 'laws', simple 'givens', or inducted rules, or categories.

If dialectical reason exists, it can only be, from the ontological point of view, the synthesis of a multiplicity into a whole, that is, a *totalization*: and, from the epistemological point of view, the permeability of this totalization to knowledge, where the act of knowing is itself totalizing. The dialectic is a totalizing activity: the relation of unifying unification (the act of knowing) to the unified unification (the object known).

The fundamental intelligibility of dialectical reason, then, if it exists, is that of a *totalization*. Hence the fundamental question of critical experience is: does there exist a sector of being where totalization is the very form of existence?

A *totality* and a *totalization* must be clearly distinguished. A totality is done, completed. The synthetic unity which produces the appearance of a totality can only be the sediment or vestige of a past act; there are so many pseudo-inert totalities: they weigh on our destiny by the contradiction of praxis (the work that has made them) and inertia (the work they put to work to maintain themselves).

The critical experience is within a totalization: it is itself both totalizing act and its own totalization, the multiplicity it is in process of synthesizing into a unified object. The act of totalization cannot be autonomous from, or external to, that which it totalizes. It is a real moment in ongoing totalization, in so far as this is incarnated in all its parts and is realized as synthetic knowledge of itself. The critical experience of the dialectic in action is therefore an experience of the dialectic interplay of the act of synthesizing, and the synthesis thus constituted, of the inextricable bond between the totalization created and the act of its creation. Thus the experience of the dialectic relation between the knower and the known is itself a dialectical experience.

The sector of being where totalization is the very form of existence is human history.

If totalization is in progress in some sector of being, this totalization can be only a single adventure in singular conditions: it produces the universals that illumine it, and it singularizes them and interiorizes them. One may speak then of *singularized universals*. Critical experience can be only a moment of this adventure. This totalizing adventure produces itself as critical experience of itself at a certain moment of its development. Abstraction, universalization, formal extrapolation, these must be singularized in the discovery of the singularity of the totalizing adventure.

When you question a single human existence, do not question

consciousness, question the individual's life, his objective being in the world of the others, in so far as he totalizes himself from birth, and will do so until death. The individual investigator who questions the totality of *all* human beings, of history itself, in this very act of thinking history is revealing a totalization being totalized and detotalized.

History always has to be rewritten, that is, detotalized and re-totalized. For history as a totalization is perpetually out of date. It will never be completed until time may have a stop. Here, the individual is the only possible methodological point of departure. Through his praxis, the dialectic is not the outcome of history, it is the original movement of its totalization by him on the basis of its totalization of him.

Thus it is not only a sector of reality characterized by totalizations that must always and everywhere be intelligible, but the totalizing movement itself. Herein consists the translucency of dialectical reason: its second intelligibility.

That is, critical experience cannot be established without its own intention, namely, the perpetual reorganization of the given in terms of acts illumined by their ends. If we wish to look at the object without this intention we can do so. Nothing prevents us from congealing and transforming men into things and human groups into mechanical systems. By such synthetic transformation and deformation, whereby we constrict and congeal dialectic experience, we are left in a pseudo-monism of subjectivism or objectivism, so that the world is swallowed up by us, or we are swallowed up by the world. Within this estranged experience, and by thinking in this estranged way, we shall certainly not discover our dialectically critical experience. But why this is the case can be made intelligible, as we have just tried to do in outline, in the light of our critical dialectical experience.

Now, if history is totalization, and if individual praxes are the unique basis of totalizing temporalization, it is necessary to ask how a multiplicity of individuals produce a praxis of a kind through a multiplicity of totalizations. One wishes for an Ariadne's thread to conduct one from individual praxes to the diverse forms of human collectives. We shall try to trace the dialectical intelligibility of these transformations, whereby praxis become praxis-process. The individual agent enters into very different collectivities. We shall have to follow the vicissitudes and transformations of praxis from series to groups to series: we shall study groups of groups: class and the being of class. While we may take examples from the working class or the bourgeoisie, it is not the primary intention of this study to define these, or any, particular classes, but rather to work out the way a class is constituted, its totalization and detotalization, and, all the time, its dialectical intelligibility, involving links of interiority and exteriority, its internal structures, relations with other classes, etc.

Above all, the aim is to recompose the intelligibility of historical movement in the interior of which different multiplicities of men come to be defined by the form of their conflicts. Starting from synchronic structures and their contradictions, we shall progress to the diachronic intelligibility of historical transformations. That is, our procedure is a synthetic progression, by means of dialectical reason as the constitutive and constituted reason of practical multiplicities. Fact, intelligibility, and necessity are to be discovered at every step.

The two volumes together try to show that necessity, as apodictic structure of dialectical experience, resides neither in the free development of interiority, nor in the inert dispersion of exteriority: it is imposed by virtue of *an irreducible and inevitable moment in the interiorization of the exterior and in the exteriorization of the interior*. Necessity is a seal, a stamp, imprinted on our subjectivity, as the condemnation that obliges us to realize freely and by ourselves the sentence that a society has passed on us, and that defines us thereby.

A regressive moment takes us from what Sartre terms the constitutive dialectic to the anti-dialectic and constituted dialectic. A progressive moment reveals the totalizing movement that integrates these three partial movements at the heart of a total totalization. Truth is revealed as the praxis of this synthetic unification. This is history.

In the following, when praxis can be linked to the intention of an organism or group, then Sartre calls it comprehensible. But it can still be regarded as intelligible if alienation has divorced action and intention too far for action to be comprehensible in terms of the intention of an identifiable agent. Sartre leads us through the exploration of different critical experiences to discover actions without apparent agents, productions without producers, totalizations without totalizators, contra-finalities, infernal circularities. Human groups, those strange practical multiplicities, will produce acts and totalized thoughts, without the individuals who comprise them being consulted, or even knowing about them. In society there are, so to say, free-floating actions, vagabonds without authors.

BOOK I

From individual praxis to the practico-inert

A. INDIVIDUAL PRAXIS AS TOTALIZATION

If the dialectic is possible, four questions follow:
1. What is the nature of praxis as experience of necessity and of freedom?
2. How are totalities totalized?
3. What is historical future?
4. What is the materiality of praxis and of other forms of materiality?

Man is mediated by things to the same extent as things are mediated by man. This is an example of the circularity of dialectical thinking. It is not a truth, but the type of thought we must have if the human scene is to be intelligible, and, as we have said, this intelligibility is primarily a question of understanding the way in which a plurality is constituted as a total—as a whole, whether as a whole subject or as a whole object: a totalization is a unifying organization of a plurality, and the human scene is a plurality of such organizations. In all this, who totalizes what?

The original totalizing relation of this material being, a man, with the material world of which he is part is defined as *need*. Need is an interiorization by the man-in-need of a lack in the exterior total field of satisfactions. Something is lacking or missing or scarce. There is not enough. I have not got something. There is a lack there of what I have not got here. Need detotalizes the full, indifferent, persisting totality of the inorganic. This detotalization, the injection of nothing into the world, is a univocal, non-reciprocal relation. By the liquidation of each partial moment, a dialectical logic of totalizations (that is, of detotalization-retotalization of the always elusive totality of the world) is set in motion. The field of my praxis is totalized, therefore, as unity of resources and means, to satisfy needs: this field is an inert plurality of resources and means, grasped as the unity of an instrumental field. Praxis alone determines the zones, systems, privileged objects in this totality, inert in itself. The body is perpetually in need so far as it functions at all. The body is function, function is need, need is praxis. Praxis as need is work: that is, the dialectic of human organic praxis and the inorganic. Analytic reason can grasp only one moment of this dialectic at a time. When we grasp this from moment to moment, we are using dialectical reason to understand a dialectical situation.

B. HUMAN RELATIONS AS MEDIATION BETWEEN DIFFERENT SECTORS OF MATERIALITY

The solitary worker, the man-in-need in relation to the inorganic non-human environment, is, of course, an abstraction. Man is always related to materiality in and through other men. That is, human relations mediate the material field we have just been describing. Put in another way, this field has always a polyvalent set of significations to a number of men. This means that the relations of individuals as in turn mediated in and through this material field are passively undergone, conditioned by external forces. As such, in one moment of the dialectic the relations between men are a function of, and are conditioned by, the inhuman.

Now, at this point one must be very clear in distinguishing material circumstances as conditions of praxis from the material world of my possibilities, that is, what I make of these conditions through my singular totalization of them by my project, that is, by my transcendence of them. At this moment of the dialectic, matter is transmuted into a vehicle of meaning. However, this circulating, inert materiality inevitably eludes me and escapes me, since it is subject to a multiplicity of other unifications or totalizations by other men, that complement my own or do not. My totalization of my field of praxis is then detotalized by being the field for a totalization of another's praxis, in which I am merely a part in his totalization.

In order to consider what is entailed by the dispersion of human organisms, Sartre invites us to contemplate two individuals entirely separated from each other, e.g. a road-mender and a gardener, unknown to each other, on either side of a wall, each observed simultaneously by me. I can comprehend each of them up to a point on the basis of a complicity, so to say, in the enterprise of each. Each person is a centre of another orientation to the objective world, a centre of another arrangement of the universe. Road-mender or gardener, each is made by what he himself does. Each is a product of his product. I can realize, unbeknown to them, the permanent possibility of their relationship. I can see, through what they do, what are the unifications that characterize their fields. Yet the plurality of these two other centres of unifications is a permanent 'elsewhere' that eludes me, although the only relationship they have with each other at the time of my present contemplation of them is mediated by me. Their relation to each other cannot be described as more than reciprocal ignorance, and this requires a third to mediate it. They can be, and are necessarily, unified in a totalization which is not theirs.

Now, reciprocal and triadic relations are the starting-point or basis of all relations including all forms of reification and alienation. Complete reciprocity would be possible only in an ideal city of ends, and it is clearly impossible *a priori* in the actual world which *a priori* is not this ideal city.

Reciprocity can be positive or negative. In reciprocity, each may make himself a vehicle of the other's project, so that the other will make himself a vehicle of one's own. Then there will be two separate transcendent ends and the reciprocity will have the character of an *exchange*. Or each makes himself the means of the other for one joint end, which will be unique and transcendent. I recognize the other both as the means towards a transcendent end of my own, and as a generator of a project for which I am a means. That is, I see him as an agent of a totalization in his movement towards his ends in the same movement as that whereby I project myself towards my own; and I discover myself to be object and instrument for his ends by the same act whereby I constitute him as object and instrument for my ends.

If there is a refusal of reciprocity, each refuses to serve the end of the other, and by recognizing his being as an objective means in the project of the other as adversary, he puts to profit his own instrumentality for the other, to make of him an instrument of his own ends: this is struggle or conflict. Each may use his own materiality to act on that of the other: each, by shamming, ruses, frauds, manoeuvres of every conceivable kind, may allow himself to be constituted by the other as a false object, as a deceptive, deceiving means to his ends. In such a struggle, the end is not to annihilate the other, to pursue the death of another, as Hegel maintains. This concrete antagonism is based on scarcity: its real end is objective *conquest*.

The contradiction of man related to man consists in the fact that his relation to the other is a totalization which must be totalized by that which it totalizes. Each member of a dyad can possess two equivalent systems of reference and two equivalent actions: but neither can realize the unity of the dyad. In the mutual recognition that operates in and through these two synthetic totalizations is found indeed the limit of unification. In mutual *respect* these remain *two* agents, each of whom integrates the entire universe. Even intimacy, by the very need for closeness, is negation of distance, and a perpetual negation of unity. Hegel has suppressed matter as the mediator between individuals. The disappearance of the adversary is only a means, not a necessary end. The 'work' of the dyad, the reciprocal adaptation of each to each, approach and withdrawal, the body as instrument,

common tasks, mutual interests, are real enough; but the unity of
the two that is negated by each is objectively possible only through
the permanent mediation of the things each uses.

It is the 'third parties' who unify the dyad, through the mediation of materiality. The inanimate is an imperative. The class of
objects and their use transform the people who use them, and
determine the given form of their relationship. By using this
machine this man is made a worker of this particular kind. In the
factory, the product is crystallization of anonymous work.

In recognition and respect the co-essentiality of the other is
affirmed. In each there is constituted the absolute interiority of a
relationship without unity except through the separate interiority
of each. As has been said, the unity of the dyad can be realized
only in the totalization operated from outside by a third. The
reciprocal relation of the dyad *per se* is haunted by its unity, that
is, by the presence of its absence, by the insufficiency of its being.
The other (as third) is the non-reciprocal mediator of the unification of the dyad. The totalization of the dyad by the thirds as it is
interiorized by each member of the dyad may indeed appear to
swallow both of them up in a purely dyadic situation (two boxers
dominated by fight), but this is a fugitive unity, a double totalization by each of the dyad as it exists *for a third party* as an object-
totality: the unity of the dyad comes to each from the presence
of the third.

The non-unity of the dyad in itself can be hidden also by the
gleam of a common task—the common rhythm of the oarsmen,
the shared chronometric time-schedule of a factory, etc. This can
obscure the heterogeneity of the dyad, which, however, remains
irreducible.

In general, the attempt by one or both members of a dyad to
interiorize the third can achieve necessarily only a sort of congealed revelation. The unity provided by the third is an imprint,
a stamp, a seal, determined by the third, and his dyadic metamorphosis by interior transformation leaves him transcendent. In
any triad, of course, *the same individual* may be engaged in

reciprocal dyadic action and at the same time may be a third to the other two, and so on. To conceive of these movements in their intelligibility, we have to be able to move from praxis as the radical unification of the field of action, to the negation of human plurality giving the fugitive unity of the dyad, from the negation of such fugitive unity by plurality to the inter-changing reciprocities of the triad.

In any event, totalization is always mediated by matter. Praxis totalizes the environment, and only through the medium of matter can human relations be totalized. This totalization of human relations is at once totalization done to matter by human relations as one moment, and totalization in a sense done to human relations by matter as another moment. Whether one moment is taken to be first or second depends on one's choice of starting-point, since the dialectic is always a spiral.

C. MATTER AS TOTALIZED TOTALITY AND A FIRST EXPERIENCE OF NECESSITY

1. *Scarcity and mode of production*

Human history is not just a dead past but its totalization by us in the present as part of our orientation of ourselves towards the future. It is the choice of what we remember, the totalizing conservation of the past in the present, as the filter through which anything of the past reaches the man of the present and future. In so far as inorganic matter is the negation of man, and yet is the condition of the possibility of the totalizing unity of history, man meets man through the negation of man. History grasped at this level has a terrible and desperate aspect—men united by this inert and demoniacal negation that takes their substance, to return it against all under the form of active inertia—the totalization of man by his extermination.

The relation of a multiplicity of individuals to the field of praxis consists, as we have seen, at once of each person's own relation to the field, and of the reciprocities between them.

At this point we must try to understand the nature of the relation of the material field to many of the passive actions, as it were, whereby materiality exercises power over men, in returning to them the praxis that they have put into it, but now as though stolen from them and coming back to them as a contra-finality, as an end that contradicts the ends of man—by the threat of extermination. This dialectic is lost in simplistic Marxism. Men not only find themselves pitted against nature, against the social milieu, against other men, they find their own praxis turns against them to become anti-praxis. This primal alienation is expressed in and through other forms of alienation, but it is independent of them, and is the basis, or condition, of the others.

Whether the relation is man to man, or man to matter, the fundamental relation in our history is the reciprocal of need-scarcity. It is the contingent determination of our univocal relation to materiality. Scarcity in the material world is constituted by need. This dialectic can also be viewed starting from scarcity, not from need. We can start from the other side of the circle, as it were. Scarcity is the basis of the possibility of our history, not its concrete reality. Other factors are necessary to produce history, and there could be other possible histories without scarcity. There could even be societies without history, based on repetition. History is born from an abrupt disequilibrium which fissures society at all levels. History is not necessary or essential. The legendary history of some tribes is the negation of history, and we still see the reintroduction of the timeless archetype at sacred moments of repetition. But if history exists, it is necessarily dialectical, and requires a dialectical examination.

Scarcity determines that, for each, all the world exists as object of consumption. As such, it constitutes the negative unity of the multiplicity of men. The utilization of the object *here* and *now* prevents its use *there* and now or then. Scarcity makes real the impossibility of co-essential existence. Under the empire of scarcity, human beings are seen as excess, as future consumers, as unnecessary at least, as a threat more fundamentally. Men are seen as quantities, and as interchangeable. Man is put in question in his being, each is one-too-many. Each man exists as inhuman, as a strange species, as other than me. The other is a risk for me. I am a risk for the other.

And men devour not only the inanimate world, and destroy each other, but they consume animals. One can, doubtless, be needlessly cruel to a particular animal, but it is in the name of human reason that this cruelty is blamed or punished. Man, this flesh-eating species who sets up hundreds of millions of beasts, either to kill them or to use their power to do his work, who destroys as many others systematically, for hygienic reasons, for self-protection, or for sport! Who could imagine that it is in the name of human reason that a man is punished for cruelty to an animal? Perhaps the thought is of his kindness to the animal he domesticates and tames in pursuit of a simplistic symbolism.

Where reciprocity is modified by scarcity, the other is seen as excess, redundant, as the contra-man, the anti-man, another species. We see his actions, and these are the actions of the anti-man, our demonic double. We see that nothing, neither the great wild beasts nor microbes, can be more terrible for man than an intelligent flesh-eating cruel species, who understands and thwarts human intelligence, and whose end is the destruction of man.

Abstract, pure, unmediated reciprocity is ruptured, therefore, by interiorized scarcity. Need and scarcity determine the Manicheistic basis of action and morals. Violence and counter-violence are perhaps contingencies, but they are contingent necessities, and the imperative consequence of any attempt to destroy this inhumanity is that in destroying in the adversary the inhumanity of the contra-man, I can only destroy in him the humanity of man, and realize in me his inhumanity. Whether I kill, torture, enslave, or simply mystify, my aim is to suppress his freedom—it is an alien force, *de trop*. As long as scarcity remains our destiny, evil is irremediable, and this must be the basic to our ethic. The negative unity of interiorized scarcity in the dehumanization of reciprocity is re-exteriorized for us all in the unity of the world as common field of our oppositions, as the contradictory unity of multiple contradictory totalizations, and this unity we in turn reinteriorize in a new negative unity. We are united by the fact of living in the whole world as defined by scarcity.

The individual himself is then, simultaneously, redundant and scarce, within the group. Scarcity must always be specified in its particular circumstances. Only careful research can determine the different contexts wherein scarcity is the condition of the possibility of history. In speaking of scarcity, some Marxists can often be quite dogmatic. Engels is often unintelligible and ambiguous. A form of scarcity they characteristically neglect, for instance, is the scarcity of time.

In short, scarcity as the negation in man of man by matter is a principle of dialectic intelligibility. Man sees his action stolen and deformed by the world in which he registers himself. Scarcity is fundamental for the understanding of our history. It remains, however, a contingency. Alienation in its two primary forms of *alteration* and *objectification* (see p. 118) is an *a priori* necessity. Matter upon which work has been done bears the stamp of man. It is his objectification. But matter further alienates in itself the act that has done work on it, not purely as force or purely as inertia, but through its inertia it returns to each the force of the work of the other.

The capitalist process as one of the possible moments of alienation reveals the domination of matter (product) by man (the worker), and the domination of man by matter *through other men*, since his own product renders him unnecessary to the others, for whom he is then redundant.

2. *Worked-on matter as alienated objectification of collective and individual praxis*

Praxis is the instrumentalization of material reality, that is, it turns matter into an instrument for human ends. It envelops the inanimate thing in a totalizing project, and imposes on it a pseudo-organic unity. One can liken this to the act of affixing a seal, of placing one's imprint on the world, and one sees, for instance, in the deforestation of the plains by the Chinese, how, by so doing, the worker can become his own material fatality, in that he produces the inundations that ruin him. Under this rubric, nature is the external limit to society. Man becomes anti-physis: matter, inverted praxis or anti-praxis. We see this also in the fetishization of matter in the history of precious metals. In the importation of gold to Spain (Philip II) there are two types of human mediation: the one communal, deliberated, synthetic, uniting man, whether exploited or not, in a common project; the other a *serial* mediation—men turn against each other, each finds the other against him in his effort to acquire the gold which in its fetishized form is now scarce, and needed. For the praxis that has gone into the gold market invests gold with its scarcity. Hence the idea of its scarcity is produced as a social fact.

Social facts are things, to the extent that all things are social facts. No matter, gold or any other, has, or is, Being, pure of signification. We must recognise in these dialectical considerations of man and matter that certain automations and certain social processes seem impenetrable to our understanding. There is an anti-dialectical limit that we come up against. But we will find no intelligible basis for praxis if we see praxis itself only as an inessential moment in a radically inhuman process.

Every philosophy that subordinates the human to Being other than man, whether existential idealism (Heidegger) or dogmatic Marxism, has as its basis and consequence the hatred of man. The basic question is: is man first himself then other, or first other then himself? Alienation can exist only if man is first praxis and is then alienated. In the same way, the precondition of slavery is the freedom that is enslaved. Man lives in a universe where the future has become a thing, the idea a social fact. But this is intelligible as alienation, and alienation is intelligible as praxis estranged by praxis. Man is himself a material reality, and he is that material reality whereby matter receives its human functions and significations.

Matter, *in and through man*, is the motor of history, and constitutes a common future. As the stone gods, the tablets, the relics of past objectified praxis, matter is the social memory of a collectivity, a transcendent yet interior unity, a totality made by a multiplicity of dispersed activities. It is the congealed menace of the future (the stock-pile of bombs). It binds men by providing the link between them, this link whereby in objectifying myself, I become another for the other.

Praxis as unification of inorganic plurality confers on matter a practical unity. Man as product of his product is in an indissoluble symbiosis with matter. So far we have considered man as praxis, himself in need, and himself an object needed, that is, a scarcity. We must remember however that in so far as he is dominated by matter man does not act simply from need, but in response to the practical demands that the inanimate object may be felt to make on him. When such demands impinge on man, they are active and not merely passive demands. So far, also, we have considered materiality as mediating the living relations between men. In complex groups, of course, divisions, separations, rigidities, fill the living links between men by a mechanical ordinance. This latter situation is on a much further level of concreteness that cannot become intelligible until later.

By the theft of his praxis through matter and the praxis of others, man's destiny becomes mechanical fatality, caught in the hell of the revolving field of practical passivity. The contradiction of class-interest, in the Marxist sense, is revealed in the individual or collective attempt to find the original and univocal link from man to matter, that is to say, to rediscover oneself as free constituting praxis; but interest is already both self-deviation and the petrification by matter of this attempt.

3. *Necessity as new structure of dialectic experience*

The only concrete basis of an historical dialectic is the dialectical structure of individual actions.

There are two forms of necessity given in the dialectical structure of human interaction that we must consider. They are both types of alienation, and Sartre regards them both as primary, since they are necessary *a priori*. He calls them *alteration* and *objectification*. Both, especially alteration, are insufficiently recognized by the Marxist dogmatist, and the theoretical implications of their necessary character have likewise been missed.

Necessity and constraint should not be confused. The basic practical experience of necessity must be through action without constraint. One form of such action without constraint is the very simplest occasion when one does something in relation to another. In no case is the result ever identical with the intention of the agent. For an *alteration* occurs when my action passes from my-action-for-me to my-action-for-you. From being mine-for-me it becomes other-for-the-other. The structural aspect of the transition to and fro from self-for-self to other-for-other Sartre calls *alterity*, and the movement he calls *alteration*. One sees that, given a relation of the type that human interaction is, alteration is a necessary feature of it. Necessity is given in experience also, when worked-on matter robs us of our action, not in so far as it is pure materiality, but as materialized praxis. This form of necessary alienation has already been discussed in the preceding section. Man acts on matter and totalized matter acts on man. Whether through *alteration*, or *objectification* into materialized praxis, the resultant is always more or less other than the intention.[1] Yet man is only encountered as his objectifications, and in his alterations, as other for another.

We shall see later, in the changing context of the different forms of practical unifications of multiplicity, namely, the groups that Sartre describes—the series, the group-in-fusion, the pledged group, the organization, the institution—that these two aspects of primary alienation are not induced by external constraints. The elementary experience of necessity is that of a retroactive power

[1] Even though result as far as one knows, and intention as far as one is reflectively aware, may often coincide nearly enough for certain practical purposes.

that nibbles my freedom from the objective finality of my act to the original decision which gave it birth. This negation of freedom at the heart of freedom, this *primary alienation* (objectification and alteration) is to be distinguished from alienation in the Marxist sense, which begins with exploitation.

Each of us passes his life engraving his malefic imago on other persons and on things. This graven image, fascinating and maddening if one wishes to be understood or to understand oneself by it, is also the very necessity of my freedom as totalization-in-movement which ends in objectification and alteration.

4. *Social being as materiality and, particularly, the being of class*

The alienation of one's praxis through alteration and objectification being-other-for-other and being-outside-in-the-Thing, is nevertheless one's truth and reality. This being-outside (*être dehors*) constitutes itself, or is constituted, as practico-inert matter. Human praxis, in so far as it is subject to matter, can fall into social impotence, into inertia. As Marx has shown, capitalism is an antisocial force: it massifies and serializes men. In the social field men are totalized by the mode of production.

Now, existentialism denies the existence of pre-formed human essences. One *is* not a coward or a thief. Can one then say that one is made bourgeois? Without doubt. Cowardice, courage, are simply convenient *résumés* of the sedimentation of complex activities. There is no comparison between them and the trappings of class. These class encumbrances can be seen variously as the passive synthesis of materiality, the crystallized praxes of preceding generations, the general conditions of social activity, the most immediate and brutal aspects of our objective reality, its predetermination in general. The life-course of a worker at Dop Shampoos, even down to the fantasies of the machinist, is predetermined in general. The factory girl, in her sexual relations, pregnancies, abortions, *realizes* by herself what she is *already*. She passes against herself the sentence already passed by the whole nexus of socio-economic conditions into which she has been born.

To transcend the conditions of one's class entails a fuller and fuller realization of them. One's being *classé* is one's prefabricated future. In this, it is a negative determination of temporalization. It is an inertia that has taken hold inside us, and if it has, then it is only through this very inertia that praxis must realize itself, and finally recognize itself in a new experience of necessity. This inertia, interiorized in each, affects the destiny, intent, exigence of each, and the structures of class values as common limits are of course a *collective* inertia, the interiorization of an inorganic materiality shared by all the individuals in its field. This collection of structures of the practico-inert field that the worker is *in* is not, however, any gelatinous reality, vaguely haunted by some supra-individual 'class consciousness'.

D. COLLECTIVES

All social objects of social study have a collective structure, and as such are studied by sociology. Sartre sees these as material beings, already products of human work, and ultimately the realities of praxis, in so far as they realize in and through themselves the inter-penetration in them of a multiplicity of organized individuals.

A group is an enterprise in a constant movement of integration. But just as the individual can be defined only by what he has done, so the collective is defined in its *being*, in so far as all praxis is converted to *exis*.[1] In this light, a group can be seen as a *material and inorganic object of the social field*. By means of a group, a discrete multiplicity of acting individuals can produce through their concerted action a type of being which they constitute as a unity. This unity, however, in achieving any degree of permanence, takes on a curious inertia born of a secondary passive synthesis as each individual praxis becomes, as it were, suffused by the passive, inert givenness of the group as a form of practico-inertia.

We are at a new moment of the spiral. We discover the same

---

[1] *Exis:* Sartre uses the Greek term ἕξις: being in a certain state, a permanent condition.

terms enriched by further partial totalizations and more reciprocal conditions. We have the following elements, to be synthesized into a new form of intelligibility. Reciprocity as fundamental human relation; separation of individual organisms; the field of praxis with its dimensions of alterity in depth; inorganic materiality, both as being-beyond-itself of man in the object, and as being-beyond-itself of the inert as exigence in man.

In so far as, in a reciprocal relation in Sartre's sense, I include you in my totalization, and you include my totalization of you in your totalization of me, and I totalize in turn your totalization of my totalization of you, and so on, a reciprocal relation can be called a relation of interiority. Such a relation of interiority contrasts with a relation of exteriority, which is simply one of two objects external to each other. Two human beings as two centres of totalizations, and as two separate organisms outside each other, are simultaneously related by interiority and exteriority. The first steps in understanding the formation of human collectivities must consist in following out the simplest ways in which some sort of resolution occurs between the opposition of reciprocity, as relation of interiority, and solitude of organisms, as relation of exteriority. As always in the spiral of the dialectic, such a resolution forms the basis of a new type of internal-external relation. This is what Sartre calls *seriality*.

A collection of people characterized by seriality will be called a *series*. The transformation of a multiplicity into a series will be called *serialization*. Consider a group of persons waiting for a bus. Their relatedness can be seen in terms of solitude, of reciprocity, of unification and massification from outside themselves. They are a plurality of solitudes. The solitude of each is not an inert necessity, but it is lived in the project of each as its negative structure: I have nothing to do with you. It is the provisional negation by each of their possible reciprocal relations. This plurality of separations is the negative side of the integration of each individual to his own separate group (bank-clerk, housewife, etc.). The girl in a hurry on her way to the office, the man absorbed in his newspaper, and the other members of the queue, are all in their own worlds, and they live their present relationship with each other as members of the queue negatively, that is, they take no notice of each other except as a number in a quantitative series. They reciprocally deny any link between each of their inner worlds. The conduct of each expresses the particular solitude of each, as the exteriorized negation of any reciprocity of interiority lived in the interior heart of the social.

These solitudes are the real social product of the city. The city is present as the interchangeability of men. The city is there already in the morning as this or that demand, or as something I can use, or as a milieu to be in. It refracts my polyvalent solitude with the million facets of the solitudes of all the people I am not in relation with. Solitude is a project. For instance, to isolate oneself by reading a newspaper is to utilize the national collective, and finally the totality of living men, to separate oneself from the ten persons who are in the same queue. Solitude, then, is at different moments, in different lights, organic; endured; lived, as imposed on me; project, as what I do. I realize my particular solitude through my conduct, and the bus queue is a reciprocity of isolations, for through the project of solitude of each, reciprocity exists as denied. Solitude, then, is the first characteristic of seriality.

The persons in a serial group are further characterized by their interchangeability. They are identical in their separation. All the members of the bus queue have a future object in common. In so far as this is so, each is the same as the other. Each is the same as the other in a further respect, in that, as well as identity in interchangeability, and separation, there is identity as alterity: the other that each is for the other is the same. Each is one too many.

A material object, the bus, determines this serial order, since there may not be room for all. Each is *redundant* for the other. It is impossible, however, to decide who specifically is redundant on any *a priori* basis, or by any intrinsic qualities of the individual. In the series alterity is unmitigated, as it were. Each is other for the other in so far as he is other. No one possesses in himself the reason for his ordinal position in the serial order. Each is identical to the other in so far as he is made, by the others, an other acting on the others. The series is only intelligible through a grasp of the formal universal structure of *alterity*.

The thing (the bus) as the being that is common to each of the series, produces the series as its own practico-inert-being-beyond-itself in the plurality of practical organisms. The series is everywhere and always constituted starting from such a common object. There are serial ways of behaving, serial feelings, serial thoughts, *The series is a mode of being of individuals*. This mode of being metamorphoses the serial individuals in all their structures. Sartre seeks to show that in all non-serial praxis there is some element of the practico-inert structure of seriality.

We said that a series finds its tentative unity in an object held in common by each member of the series. In a multiplicity, under particular circumstances, *the Other* may become the being held in common by all. This serial Other is a practico-inert object. The other is me in every other, and every other in me, and each as other in all the others. In any event, *the unity of the series is always elsewhere*. When this serial alterity is itself the bond of the series, the whole is a totalization of flight.

The Jew, *the* petit bourgeois, *the* manual worker—are not merely concepts, but *beings*—they are unitary objects posited by and uniting serial groups. *The* Jew is not *the type* common to each particular example—but the perpetual being-beyond-himself in the other. 'The Jews' is a practico-inert grouping constituted as such by the anti-Jews.[1]

The members of a series are appendages, as it were, of their common fantasy object.

The serial collectivity, then, is a totalization, a form of social relations which supposes an original synthetic praxis, whose end is the human production of unity as its objectification in and through man. The totality of the series (e.g. the anti-Semites) is

[1] That is, its being is like the being of the bus to the queue, and the anti-Semites are a *series* united by the 'object' they have in common—namely, the Jews.

only the passive action of a practico-inert object (the Semites) on a dispersion—the seal, stamp, imprint, of exteriority revealed in the interiority of social relations. It sets up a false reciprocity between the material object and the multiplicity of human beings.

The anti-Semites are a multiplicity of men. What they have in common is a common object—the Jews. 'The Jews' for each anti-Jew is his own anti-self. Each anti-Semite recognizes his identity with the others who have anti-selves in common with him. This common bad object is a stamp or mark common to all the anti-Semites. This bad object is their badge or symbol of unification. But this unification is the unification of a series: that is, of a multiplicity in which each is identical, interchangeable, inessential, separate, and solitary.[1]

The foregoing explication of part of the rationality of alterity has given us principles for an understanding of *the practico-inert social field*. Such *practico-inert social fields* are very common, and vary with the way each person is present to the others. Real presence can occur in a telephone conversation. But the listeners to a radio programme can have only an indirect presence to each other. No common praxis between them is therefore possible. Yet, in listening to the radio, I am somehow in the presence of the other listeners. For instance, in irritation at some phoney propaganda, I turn off the radio to stop the *others* hearing it. This serial presence, united by the common being of the programme, and dispersed, impotent, separated, yet under the spell of alterity, is exploited by all mass media of advertising and propaganda. Alterity gives us the rationality of scandal, of the series that the readers of the newspaper make up.

The social field of the series is the unity of otherness, of a quasi-plurality. It is always receding, a unity as absent. The totality of the others is the milieu and general conditioning factor of serial conduct. This receding totality is not, however, a positive and

[1] It must be remembered that Sartre is here not describing a concrete group. He is showing that seriality is one aspect of the concrete reality of 'anti-Semites'.

concrete totality with a real presence. It is not the resultant of genuine unification of a field. It is a real extrapolation of an infinite series of links identical and other, in so far as each conditions the other by its absence. Serial unity is a negative totality. The international stock-exchange gives a further example of this.

The serial object, while being the being common to each member of the series, and hence the condition of its unity, is in fact the index of separation of its members. A public opinion poll is an index of lack of community.

When a social class is seen in terms of the practico-inert field, one sees that it is largely a series, and the being-of-class is to some extent the *statut*[1] of seriality imposed on the multiplicity who compose it.

The serial *idea* is not a conscious moment of action, that is, a unifying revelation of objects in the dialectical temporalization of the action, but is a practico-inert object. The evidence of a serial idea is in my double incapacity to verify it or to transform it in the others. Its opacity, my powerlessness to change it in the other, my own and the other's lack of doubt about it, are offered as evidence of its truth. The ideas of racialism and colonialism are such serial ideas.

Marx, in *Capital*, spoke of the atomization, reification, and separation of men. He showed clearly how the combined efforts of individuals cannot recur in the serialized collective. The struggle of the worker in nineteenth-century capitalism was against his destiny as a common inertia. The negation necessary for him if he was to be a man, was of his destiny as a practico-inert common object, the negation, that is, of the multiplicity-as-series of which he was one unit. This negation is the beginning of dialectical experience.

[1] Once a certain form of relatedness has been constituted, certain general consequences follow from the ontological structure of this particular form of sociality. The term *statut* denotes that array of necessary consequences that follow when one presupposes a particular form of sociality as one's starting-point. Thus a social system having been constituted, its constitution can be conceived as the starting-point for a second dialectical movement, or set of movements, which occurs under the statute or ordinance of the particular system constituted.

What can be the rigorous rationality, the dialectical intelligibility of this field of the practico-inert—this place of violence, of shadows, of sorcery? One thing is clear; there is no force that moves somehow from individual to series to common action.

There are in fact *two dialectics*: that of the individual praxis, and that of the group as praxis, and *the practico-inert field is the anti-dialectic of each*, that is, the practico-inert social field is negated by individual and group praxis, and is the negation both of individual action and of the praxis of the group. This is not recognized in the theory of Marx and Engels. Their mistake begins with their failure to see that all objectification is alteration. Every objectification becomes other because it is an object in the free field of action of the other. This is the freedom that limits freedom. The failure of Hegel is that he does not recognize that materiality is the necessary intermediary between two freedoms. The first alienation (by objectification and alteration) is that one praxis steals the meaning from the other, or, at least, necessarily alters it. Now, there is a univocal hence unambiguous relation of product to producer, but there is an equivocal hence possibly ambiguous relation of product to producer or buyer. Thus, through his objectification in his product the producer is possibly signified to the buyer differently than he wishes to signify by his product.

The following, therefore, is a schema for the intelligibility of praxis—practico-inert—praxis.

1. The univocal relation of interiority at the heart of the free praxis as unification of the field.
2. The equivocal relation of a multiplicity of practical activities, of which each steals the freedom of the others by the transformations which it makes their objectifications undergo. Practical activities are at the same time negative reciprocal relations, relations of interiority, and, by mediation of the inert object, indirect relations of exteriority.
3. The transformation of all free praxis into exis.
4. The transformation of each exis into passive activity by the

free praxis of the other, whose projects and perspectives are
other.

5. The transformation of each into passive activity by the passive activity of the object.

Exigence and seriality are unavoidable. We are all born into families riven by seriality. Freedom can only be the necessity of living the exigence by praxis. There is no possibility of opting out of the necessity of freedom.

In contrast to the translucent consciousness of our activity, there is the grotesque or monstrous apperception of the practico-inert, the interior inhumanity of the human. Alienation in its necessary primary forms, and the resulting opportunities for mystification, give the power to the praxis that aims at the impotence of the other, the aim being an anti-finality, whose end is to reduce the other to slavery.

The other *that I am* cannot in principle be lived in the dialectical development of praxis: it is the receding object of consciousness, and non-consciousness of itself. The *elsewhere* is therefore the spatial structure of alterity, and with this *elsewhere* (my always being other for every other) comes that common powerlessness of the series as the negative cement of all its members. Serial necessity and serial freedom are the statistical contingencies of physical laws. Necessity, as limit at the heart of freedom, as blinding evidence and moment of inversion of praxis in the activity of the practico-inert, becomes, after man has whirled away in serial sociality, the very structure of all ideas or feelings of seriality, the modality of their absence in presence and of their empty evidence. The field of the practico-inert is not a new moment of a universal dialectic, but the pure and simple negation of dialectic by exteriority and plurality. The necessity of freedom at this point is that the original dialectics of the individuals depass themselves to constitute a new dialectic which they constitute starting from the anti-dialectic as indepassable impossibility.

This brings us to the beginnings of the historical enterprise.

Since this new dialectic is constituted by that of human individuals in the first place, we shall speak of the *constitutive dialectic* (whose starting-point is the praxis of individuals) and the *constituted dialectic* (whose starting-point is the praxis of groups), both in the face of the anti-dialectical moment of the practico-inert field.

BOOK II

From the group to history

A. THE GROUP. THE EQUIVALENCE OF FREEDOM AS NECESSITY AND OF NECESSITY AS FREEDOM; LIMITS AND EXTENT OF ALL REALISTIC DIALECTIC

There is no *a priori* necessity that a multiplicity should become a group. However, one can say that the peculiar negative unity of the series, containing within its structure at least the germ of the abstract negation of seriality, provides the elementary conditions of the possibility of its members constituting a group.

Sartre now begins to consider ways in which a multiplicity of persons achieve practical unity in themselves, or are perceived by others as being a social unity. The most obvious error to be got out of the way at the beginning is organismic idealism, in terms of which the group is seen as a hyper-organism. This is based on a perceptual illusion, namely, the illusory appearance of the group as an organism when it is produced as a figure against the ground of a largely practico-inert social field. Those outside the group see the group and act towards it as if it were an organic totality. There is thus a tendency to unify this group-object as an organismic gestalt conceptually as well as perceptually.

The sole intention here is the critical one of determining the rationality of collective action, the genesis of a group, and the structures of its praxis. And when one sees the struggle within it against the practical inertia which afflicts it, one will see the group as passion.

Now, non-unified multiplicities do not necessarily precede groups historically, and when they do occur they contain at most the possibility not the necessity of a synthetic union of their members. In Sartre's view, however, the *dis*integration of a group has an intelligibility *a priori*. To fix the conditions and limits of this intelligibility he studies initially ephemeral groups that form and dissolve rapidly, and then moves progressively towards the study of the fundamental groups of society.

What is the intelligibility of the origin of the cataclysm which rends a mere collection to the heart by the illumination of a common praxis?

The meaning of reality is the impossible, the coefficient of resistance to my praxis. The transformation that my praxis demands is that the impossible becomes impossible to accept. At this moment of suffocation the impossibility of change becomes the impossibility of living.

We have seen that in the simplest form of capitalism the ensemble of the means of production belongs to the others, and that this gives to the proletariat its original structure of seriality. How does such a series become transformed into a group? What happened on the 12th of July? Then, each member of what before had been a series reacted in a new way—neither as individual nor as other, but as singular incarnation of the commune. This new reaction has nothing in it of magic—simply the re-interiorization of a lost reciprocity. At the Apocalypse there is a prophetic vision of the dissolution of the series in the *group-in-fusion*. This group is amorphous, as is the series in the abstracted forms we have so far described, but everywhere it is *here*, not elsewhere, *now*, not then.

How does a group arise through other groups or out of the dialectic of series and practico-inert?

The true problem of structural intelligibility is: in what conditions can a series—where unity is always receding from other to elsewhere—turn into a group? Is the instrumentality for this transformation in the series itself? In order to prepare an answer to this, let us look more closely at the contradiction of unity and alterity. Here we need to introduce the 'third' man, or, as we shall call him, simply 'the third'.

The third is not the totality he totalizes, but, by a threat that menaces him along with the others he is looking at, he realizes himself as integrated in the totality he totalizes. Each person as third is absorbed into the totality. This is what happens in series that panic *en masse* (contagion, etc.). The group must therefore be distinguished as the group-object and the group-subject.

It is the error of many sociologists to take the group as a binary relation (individual-community), whereas it is always ternary— each member of the group is a third—totalizing the reciprocities of each of the others, and being included in the totalizations of the others as thirds in turn. *The relation of third to third, however, is not serial.* It is a double mediation of the group between the thirds, and of each third between the group and the other thirds.

The first moment of mediation (the group as mediator between third and third) can be seen in a regrouping after a flight. A hundred men have run away. They are all cowards (their cowardice at this point being a serial sentiment). Each counts up the group. As I do so, the group grows in me and in the other, by me in the other, by the other in me.

The second mediation is given when the third is creator of an objective for the group, or is the organizer of means for the group. By giving the group something to do, I give the others a way of serving the group. The being-in-the-group of each is thus an interiority or bond of interiority mediated by the praxis of a regulating third.

We have still not answered the question, however, as to the intelligibility of the group-in-fusion. The central problem is the whirling unity of the various syntheses, of the multiplicity of unifications. Do these syntheses make *the* synthesis?

At the moment when the multiplicities of serial syntheses fuse somehow into an overall synthesis, uniting men for and by action, it has been easy for some sociologists to lapse into idealism—to postulate, in effect, a new transcendent being. But at this moment, it is each third, as himself, and not as other, who operates the syntheses, totalizations, and any unification of them, by interiorizing the totalizing designations in and through which other groups treat his group as a totality. Each third, by his synthetic activity, liquidates serial interchangeability. There is even an excess of unifications in a sense, but it is certainly not a question of some gelatinous agglutination. Without yet being able to make their fusion fully intelligible, it seems that the multiplicity of individual syntheses can form the basis of a community of objectives and actions.

In contrast to the series, which is a circularity of flight that destructures each here-now in disqualifying it by the here-now of the others, the circularity of the group-in-fusion comes from everywhere as this here-now, to constitute it the same everywhere, and at the same time, as free, real activity. The group-in-fusion is everywhere—not elsewhere. In this ubiquity, it is not that I am myself in the other—in this fused praxis there *is* no other. In the spontaneous praxis of the group-in-fusion, the praxis of each is realized by each as me everywhere. At this stage, there is no thought of co-operation or solidarity.

The multiplicity of syntheses here in question is not the inert coexistence of identical processes bound by exterior links. Nor is it a serial liaison of alterity. There is no hypersynthesis, no transcendent synthesis, no privileged synthesis of syntheses.

The unity of this fused group is in the interior of each synthesis. Each such act of synthesis is bound by reciprocal interiority with every other synthesis of the same group, in so far as it is also the interiority of every other synthesis. The unity is unification from within of the plurality of totalizations.

The intelligibility of this new structure—*unity as ubiquity here*—which is interior to each and every synthesis, rests on two basic principles:

(1) This ubiquity is a ubiquity of praxis, of acts in progress: not of a substance.

(2) This ubiquity is therefore a ubiquity of freedom: the group in fusion is the resurrection of freedom. My freedom in the

group-in-fusion is simultaneously my singularity and my ubiquity. It dissolves the elsewhere of alterity into a here-everywhere.

That is to say, the intelligibility of the group-in-fusion is given as individual praxis converting itself freely into common praxis. This can be put in various ways. It is the negation of alterity, which is itself a negation. It is the negation of the old reality of impotence, of the negation of the impossibility of being man. Each praxis presages the future, bringing terror, hope, violence. In an alienated society, freedom can only be revealed first in alienated form: as the realization of freedom develops it can no longer deny itself. Freedom is impossible, but, once realized, freedom is realized to be necessary. Freedom becomes necessary, and under the ordinance of this necessity the impossibility must be negated. The metamorphosis from series to group brings *hope* and *terror*, *freedom* and *violence*—all four are indissolubly united in all revolutionary activity.

We still know nothing of the history of the totalization of totalizations, and of the subsequent threats of disappearance of the group from within itself by dispersion or ossification (inertia).

Let us go back to examine what happens to the relationships of individuals, as totalizing and totalized, not as presence *here* as total praxis, as we have just been doing. On this level, the problem is the intelligibility of the transformation of the individual from being-in-seriality to being-in-the-group. Does group activity condition the being-in-the-group of each? What meaning must be given to these expressions? We shall see that there is the double moment of totalizing syntheses, which is demanded by the transcendence-immanence structure of the being-in-the-group of its members.

Now, remembering our basic definition of intelligibility, the group is intelligible if it has a praxis, that is, if it sets a dialectic in motion. We see that the group does in fact act in a sense. It can totalize its object, pursue a total end, unify the practico-inert field and dissolve it in the synthesis of the common practical field. That is to say, the praxis of the group is dialectical. But this group praxis is not a simple amplification of the praxis of individuals. This group praxis, through dialectical, is not the same sort of praxis as that of an individual. The group is not a hyper-individual. The fusion of the group is in fact the invention of each. That is to say, the group is *constituted* by the praxis of each practical organism. For this reason, Sartre speaks of two dialectics—the *constituted* dialectic of group praxis, and the *constituting* dialectic of individual praxis.

In my interiorization of multiplicity, in my affirmation here of my freedom as recognition of all *our* freedoms, in each totalization as constitution of the means of praxis, in the synthetic and common character of the original urgency of *our* objectification in victory—in none of the above respects is there a hyper-organism or a hyper-dialectic—the unity of the group is immanent in the multiplicity of syntheses, of which each is individual praxis, and this unity is never that of a completed, accomplished totality, but that of a totalization which is being invented here and everywhere, by me and by everyone.

Sartre now starts to consider the intelligibility of the group after it already exists (and it is necessary to bear in mind that the question is not one of any necessary temporal sequence in the genesis of actual groups). Once the group-in-fusion is in being, the intrinsic nature of its ontological status gives us various possibilities *a priori*. It is faced with unity and/or differentiation, permanence or dissolution. What are the forms of intelligibility of the various possible praxes at this point?

There is a dialectical problem of unity and differentiation. Both are traceable to praxis, but are these two praxes incompatible? This difficulty must be resolved if the group is to survive. The consciousness of the group as an entity that requires our praxis to preserve it is a new step in the transformation of each being-in-the-group towards a new form of group integration.

The survival group is first a practical invention in each of the permanence of a common unity through each other. It is freedom wishing to become inert, *praxis* seeking a way of metamorphosing itself into *exis*. When a multiplicity of freedoms makes common praxis in order to find a basis of the permanence of the group, it produces by itself a form of reciprocity mediated by its own inertia. This new form of reciprocity Sartre calls the *pledge*.[1] The pledge takes different forms. The historical act is not the necessary form of the pledge. It can be seen as the resistance of the survival group against separationist action, whether of going away or differentiation; as guarantee of the future through a lack of change produced in the group by freedom. Paradoxically, as provision of stability, as promise of permanence, and so forth, it affords the basis of all separation and differentiation. The pledge, however, is not a social contract, in Rousseau's sense, but the necessary passage from an immediate form of the group in danger of dissolution to another more reflective permanent form.

The pledge, as an invention of praxis, is the affirmation by the thirds of the permanence of the group as negation of its permanent possibility of negation through the multiplicity of alterity. The threat to the permanence of the group is, of course, not necessarily the physical extermination of its members. By the pledge the group seeks to make itself its own instrument against seriality, which threatens it with dissolution.

The pledge is not a subjective determination. *It is a real modification of the group* by my regulative action. It is my guarantee to the others that it is impossible for serial alterity to be introduced into the group through me. This guarantee cannot, however, annul the permanent possibility that I can 'freely', that is, by my individual praxis, abandon my post, go over to the enemy. Treason and desertion can never be annulled as possibilities, but I have sworn my loyalty, I have given my pledge as guarantee against this exercise of my own freedom. I seek to utilize my own and everyone else's presence in the group as a third, as regulator, as my common-being, as a fact that cannot be transcended. *I seek to convert my free being-in-the-group* into *an exigency that there is*

---

[1] *The pledge* (Fr. serment): Sartre speaks of *assermentation* and the *groupe assermenté*.

no way through or round, by the invention, as far as it is possible, of an inorganic, non-dialectical, rigid future. This rigid substantiation of my future is endowed with the triple characteristics of being the exigence, container, and ground of all my subsequent praxis. But there is no new dialectic. The permanence that has been invented is only the negative determination of the original dialectic.

Now, thus far two developments of the group-in-fusion have been distinguished for clarity—*survival group* and *pledged group*. We must now consider more closely the intelligibility of the pledge. The individual and the group praxis of the group-in-fusion have been seen to be comprehensible. Is the re-invention of the pledge in defined circumstances a process that is dialectical and comprehensible?

The pledge becomes intelligible as the common action of the group on itself. We said above that the group undergoes a transformation in and through the common action of the pledge. How then does the unity of the group-in-fusion compare with that of the pledged group? The former is a fusion in the face of material danger. In this fusion, real work is done. In the pledged group, on the other hand, nothing material binds the members, the danger is not real, it is only possible. The origin of the pledge is anxiety. Once the real menace from outside has passed, the danger to the permanence of the group is from dispersion and seriality. A reflexive fear arises.

There is not enough to fear to keep the group together now that the danger seems remote. The condition of the permanence of the group is thus the negation of the absence of fear. Fear must be reinvented. The fundamental reinvention, at the heart of the pledge, is the project of substituting a real fear, produced by the group itself, for the external fear that is becoming remote, and whose very remoteness is suspected as deceptive. And this fear as free product and corrective action of the group against serial dissolution is *terror* induced by the *violence* of common freedom. Terror is the reign in the group of absolute violence on its members.

The essential basis for this transformation is the risk of death that each runs at the heart of the group as possible agent of dispersion. The pledged group is a common product of reciprocities mediated under the statute of violence. Through this form of unification, the being-in-the-group becomes a limit that can be breached only with the certitude of dying.

Traced to original praxis, man is in the position of absolute power of man over man. But in the vicissitudes of alienation, God can be substituted for the guillotine. The pledge, the oath of loyalty, backed up by violence, is the original free attempt to strike terror into each by each, in so far as it must constantly reactualize violence as the intelligible negation of individual freedom by common praxis.

This is the pledge. Its intelligibility is complete, since it is a question of a free transcendence of elements already given, towards an objective already posited. My pledge offers him and them a guarantee and invites violence as his and their right to suppress me if I default. By the same token the unmitigated pledge creates Terror, and invents treason, since there is now no excuse for defection. While the circumstances are not particularly constraining, I can remain on a level where violence-terror, loyalty-treachery, are not experienced in ultimate form. But the fundamental structure of the pledged group is violence-terror, since I have freely consented to the possible liquidation of my person. My *right* over the other is my *obligation* to them, and contains in itself, implicitly, death as my possible destiny.

The group-as-permanence is, therefore, an instrument constructed in certain circumstances, starting from a group-in-fusion. On the level considered, the group is, first, only the impossibility for each of abandoning the common praxis: or, in each person, its being is death as the inert negation of all possibility of strictly individual action. Although the unification of terror is based on the thought 'They will do this to me if I . . .', yet this unification does not fall into seriality, since this being-other (the Them) is in each third the same being-other as in his neighbour. In this sense, violence is everywhere, and everywhere is terror. This is terror that unites, not separates. The individuals find their own terror, each in the other, as the same. It is *here* and *everywhere*.

But in the pledge group, there is liable to exist also a mortal concern for my co-member, my brother, he who is linked to me in an indissoluble bond, an eternity of presence without future. We have come out of the mud together, and now the brother, whose existence is not other than mine, depends on me as I depend on him. Let there be no mystification about having a 'common nature'. We are brothers because we are our own sons, our fraternity is our common invention. This fraternity is an ensemble of reciprocal and singular rights and obligations. The badge for group membership might be the colour of skin. This can be pledged as guarantee against possible defection as among a clan of white lynchers in the Southern States. Fraternity is always invented in particular circumstances, in a particular perspective, evoking a particular reciprocity. Given this specification, fraternity is the right of each over each, and the practical power of the bond of fraternity is nothing other than the right and obligation of each and all to each and all of violence and terror. If, for instance, one of the lynchers tries to opt out, he is in one instant no longer my brother for whom I evince mortal concern, and hate and violence are revealed as terror exercised on the traitor. Where circumstances have occasioned the invention of love as the practical bond between the lynchers, violence is the very force of this lateral reciprocity of love, and terror is the counterpart of violence, engendered and invented by the group itself.

Indeed, all the internal conduct of individuals in pledged groups (fraternity and love as well as anger and lynching) draw their terrible power from terror itself. In this sense, each is the same for each in the unity of a common praxis, but, precisely because reciprocity is not integration; because the epicentres remain, albeit dissimulated, in mediated reciprocity; because I cannot be the totalizing third without being totalized; because the other-become-me is found also in me, as me-become-other—because of all this—the possibility of constraint or extermination is given at one and the same time in each reciprocal relation.

The sacred constitutes the fundamental structure of terror as legalized power. Here belong equally heresy, revelation, prayer, adoration. Without the law as the new synthetic product issuing from the pledged group, freedom in human relations does not intimidate. In the original alienation of alteration and objectification there is a negation of each person's possibilities by the other, prior to anybody's express intention. But the pledge introduces violence as work done on my freedom by myself or others, by freely pledging my future in committing myself to an inert-future. This freely induced inertia of freedom, this negative power, is terror.

Sartre now considers organization, function, structure, and process in the group.

To summarize briefly his position so far: we know two types of intelligible action: the translucid but abstract praxis of the individual, and the rudimentary praxis of the group-in-fusion. This latter, so long as non-differentiated, can be thought of as an amplification of individual action. Without differentiated organization, the 'same' group is everywhere. The operation of fusion thus largely conserves the translucency of individual praxis. Organized actions, however, put in play such a system of relations and relations between relations, and so on, that we have to ask once more in real earnest what type of action is here manifested. To what extent is there true praxis, and to what extent is the activity of the organized group not genuine praxis but the movement of a constituted instrument?

Now organization can denote either or both:

(i) actions interior to the group whereby a group defines its structures

(ii) the group itself as structural activity, acting on the practical field, on worked-on matter, or on other groups.

We have seen, however, that the internal praxis of the pledged group reveals its external tasks laterally or tangentially, as it were, through the morphology created by the differentiation of the praxis of each third. This differentiation is not a problem, but what, if any, is the intelligibility of *organized* action? It is a question of knowing what type of unity or reality, what meaning a praxis can have under this new form of organized praxis. That is, we must link (i) and (ii) above, to ask what is the connection between the action of the group on itself with the actions of its members on the external field.

The basic elements of the ensuing section are here summarized, although this order of presentation is not strictly adhered to. The relation between the action of the group and the action of its members is studied progressively in terms of:

1. The group task as the objective of an organizational process.
2. The transformation of the individual from unorganized group-man to organized group-man. This new determination of the individual will be seen to be both a limitation and an enrichment.
3. Function as a new statute of the man of the organization. Function will be seen to have the double aspect of
   (a) practical task in relation to object
   (b) a human relation, particularly in terms of the being-in-the-group of the third.
4. The basis of a logistic of organized systems (as multiplicity and unity of inverted and mediated reciprocities).
5. Structure.
6. Finally, all our conclusions can be regrouped in a synthetic movement which will reveal the intelligibility of organized praxis, and will let us discover a new apodeicticity—i.e. a necessity radically differentiated from any encountered so far; and enable us to question the ontological status of the organized group. Has it the translucency of a practical existence or the opacity of a substantial being?

Function as an inert limit of freedom of and by each third

person is built on violence-terror. It can be seen in various perspectives. Its most univocal positive content is in terms of distribution of tasks. This affords us a positive definition of the organized individual. It is an assignation, but it is also a determination. That is, it is negative as well as positive. It is simultaneously a positive ('Do this') and a negative injunction ('Don't do something else'). As assignation-determination, its element of positive injunction ('Do precisely this') involves a *right* to do this, and an *obligation* to do it. The element of power in function is predetermined. The inertia thus implied actualizes the sovereignty of things, of non-praxis, of the power of process over men.

The intricate differentiations of functions in, say, a football team, are diachronic totalizations of the task and practical field. Function in this context can be maximally contrasted with the function of the lone pilot. In each case, however, the individual in his function has certain practical options. Each praxis of the individual in a function (whether goal-keeper or pilot), is perfectly unintelligible if one does not start from the tools, techniques, communal objectives, material circumstances at the agent's disposal. But within the limits of the function, there is necessarily a free organization of the field of praxis. Indeed, such praxis within the context of function now occurs on the basis of the enriching limitations which the function has produced. On this level, so-called individual qualities are only the history of the technical options of free dialectical agents—but metamorphosed as functionalized men, organization-men.

The individual-as-organic-praxis is on this side, as it were, of the organized individual, but in so far as the former begins to constitute himself as the latter by his pledge, he emerges differentiated as an individual limited and determined in his conduct by his self-commitment to the group. But in this new moment of his reality he is only the common ubiquitous praxis, in so far as this must be actualized by individual conduct which always potentially transcends it.

Action is irreducible: one cannot understand it without knowing the rules of the game, but in no case can it be reduced to the rules. Individual praxis, surpassing by its concrete temporalization, its specific style, the group individual per se, is found retrospectively to be modified by each other praxis (a good pass in football cannot be defined without reference to what is made of it by the others. A good pass to a bad player is not a good move). Is this alienation? The one person's praxis may or may not be validated by the others. This mediation by the other, and the mediation of this mediation, brings us to a process of serial alienation. We have come upon the schema of the moment of necessity. We remember that this schema is that the action of the practical organism in being objectified is discovered as other, as much in its practical essence as in its results. The situations are not, however, entirely similar, because in this case, in contrast to the series, the individual praxis may be fulfilled and realized through this mediation, as well as being invalidated. In the team-spirit individual praxis is mediation which effaces or negates itself, so that it can be negated or enhanced by a third. Its total and singular aim is to produce a certain result. As with the football pass, it is instantly metamorphosed into the individual praxis of another. Herein lies the possibility, in the very heart of the team-spirit, of usurpation, confiscation of power, and return to seriality. We see the spiral nature of the return to seriality at different levels of the spiral. This is the menace on this new level. The sole specific and direct action of the organized group is organization and perpetual reorganization, in other words, its action on its members. With this organization comes inevitably the reappearance of alterity.

Each of these workers, sportsmen, combatants, is my brother, in so far as his differentiated function commands and permits me to fulfil my function. But fraternity is discovered in its abstract nudity between heterogenous individuals as an immediate and fundamental relation, which subsists in the absence of a specified relation. Functional relations entail sub-ordinations and co-ordinations. The organized group is a complex circularity of mediated reciprocities. The new type of reciprocity, which is a product of group work on the original relation, reveals the first effect of this work. The fundamental relationship of the original reciprocity, once the group is pledged, is no longer direct, convergent, spontaneous. With the pledge, reciprocity is centrifugal. It is a bond sustained in the absence of the others, not only lived in their presence. Each in his solitude has guarantees and imperatives, rights and obligations. No more is there a spontaneous living invention of relatedness, but a reciprocal inertia. The heterogeneity of functions is a determination of this reciprocal inertia. Consider the situation of a doctor in a small town paying a medical visit to the Deputy Mayor just before municipal elections! Think of the intricate nexus of fixed assumption and allocation of roles through which their transaction must be mediated. Yet the inert reciprocity of functional relations, as a reciprocal inertia, can be paradoxically a sort of affirmation against emptiness and separation. It displays, as it were, an inorganic materiality of freedom.

In contrast, *when mediated reciprocities are freely determined by group praxis*, risks are being taken all the time: every relation is constantly open to modifications by secondary reactions of reciprocities developed on the basis of re-distributions and realignments of tasks.

The problem for the group that organizes itself in the light of a reflexive consciousness of its practical unity is less to neutralize or suppress by violence retroacting reciprocities, than to reappropriate them, to recoup them in the perspective of the objective consciously pursued.

There is a perpetual work that any group must exercise on itself. *The organization group is practical and living only as a progressive synthesis of a plurality of reciprocal fields*. All communal organization is multi-dimensional.

A calculus of reciprocities would be a useful task for someone to work out. The question is not whether these reciprocal multiplicities exist, for they undoubtedly do in great intricacy, but whether, or to what extent, they exist in the organized group independent of its concrete end and history. Is there an inert skeletal structure of the organization outside the terrain of praxis and dialectic, possessing a sort of inorganic necessity? The whole question of the intelligibility of organized praxis is without doubt susceptible to study by 'exact science'—we shall see shortly the limitations of this study. The curious characteristic of this skeletal structure is that it is at one and the same time inert relatedness and living praxis. *Function as lived praxis is encountered in its objectification as structure*. Structure is the objectification of function. What then is the intelligibility of structure?

STRUCTURE

According to Lévi-Strauss, in one tribe that he has studied, kinship relations are rigidly ordained by algebra. If there are two family lines, A and B, the marriage of a male of A to a female of B is (+) for the A line and (−) for the B line, and vice versa. Generally the loss of a female is (−), the gain of a female is (+). The pluses and minuses must, however, be kept even, by the imbalance in one generation being corrected in the second. The son (an A) of a husband of A and wife from B, cannot marry a B strain daughter, for instance. Quite a complicated and rigorous algebraic logic appears to be at work when it is a question of cousin and second-cousin marriages, and so on. Needless to say, the tribe is not aware of the algebra in terms of which it operates. They can only say that such and such a marriage is possible or impossible. There appears to be a completely ossified structure, which seems to be dialectically quite unintelligible.

Every individual who is born into a pledged group finds himself in a situation where pledges have already been given on his behalf. He is pledged by proxy, as it were, ahead of himself. The ordinal algebra of Lévi-Strauss becomes intelligible, Sartre states, in terms of commitments, pledges, oaths, powers, rights and obligations, and the appropriate ceremonies and rites of baptism, initiation, etc. He calls these structures in so far as their inorganic materiality, for instance, the algebra of the structures of kinship relations, has been interiorized and reworked by the group: *the necessity of freedom*. This necessity is exactly the inverse of the practico-inert so far studied. It is that on which my praxis rests, it contains, circumscribes and canalizes it. It is the needed spring-board for praxis. But praxis itself is never this skeletal structure. The group absorbs inertia in order to struggle against inertia. This active passivity is a springboard for praxis on three levels: power (freedom-terror), function (right-obligation) and inert skeleton (structure).

Now, structure has a double face. It is an analytic necessity and a synthetic power. The power is constituted by producing in each the inertia which forms the necessary springboard of praxis.

Relations within a structured group are of course mediated reciprocities.

The structure of the group becomes apparent to its members in so far as the group is quasi-object for its own members. The turning of the group into an object for its members does not turn it into a totality. It remains a totalization.

Through the very act of objectification one can see that *a unity of inertias can produce by itself no modification in anyone except by the praxis of someone*.

If structure as a form of objectification of functional praxis is not dissolved by further functional activity, it is reinteriorized: the agent realizes it in his very activity on two intersecting levels: first, as work done by the group on its own practical multiplicity, in order to concert the praxis of everyone towards a common task or mission, that is, the work of turning the group itself into an instrument: second, as the group's inertia that is also his inertia. Through his own commitment to the group he allows himself to assume within himself a quantification of himself, a quantitative identity. External structure signifies internal ossification. The multiplicity of predetermined relations is both an anti-dialectical limit of praxis and a limit that has been determined by nothing but praxis itself.

The organized totalization designates and solicits individual action as function, and constitutes it as power and instrumentality. The individual entering a group already realizes its anterior totalization as having staked out the limits for his own conduct, and in this context pursues his own totalizing operation.

Structure is the quite specific relation of the terms of a reciprocal relation: the structure, as Sartre puts it,[1] *is existed* by everyone, in and through each and every relationship. Once more, the structural mediation of each relation is *in each*, as the unity of interiorized multiplicity, and *nowhere else*. The structural relatedness in the group must now be considered in respect of the group's reflexive texture, the reflexive knowledge the group in some sense has of itself. In other words, questions about the 'ethic' and 'truth' of the group now arise.

Structure has the double character of *inert* object (a calculus if one considers it as skeleton) and effective *dynamic* actualized by the praxis of each and all. The structural idea has this same double character.

Functional relations define not only the degree of abstraction of thought but the limits of its application: the functional relational system is both an instrument of, and a limit to, the power to think. Indeed, the structural system, constituted as it is as a generalized system of logical relations, suggests that intellectual fidelity to logical principles is only one form of fidelity to the deep-seated underlying pledge of the group in question, that is, to the whole system of violence-terror, obligations-rights, functions, structures, powers, instrumentality, that characterize it.

The relational system of the skeletal structure can be studied in different ways, according to the type of analytic-synthetic rationality brought to bear on it. But one must be careful to know what one is doing. A diagram of kinship relations is a construction. It is not a thought. It is a piece of manual work controlled by a synthetic knowledge which it does not itself express. Dialectical reason sustains, controls, and justifies all other forms of thought,

[1] Using the verb 'to exist' transitively, as he has done before in *Being and Nothingness*.

since it explicates them, putting them in their true place, and integrates them as non-dialectical moments which find, thus placed in dialectical context, their dialectical validity.

Now let us once more put the scope and limits of the dialectic to the test, by the dialectical consideration of structure as system and function. In the investigation so far, be it noted, we have encountered no *critically* new problems—the pledge, fraternity—terror—violence, inertia of reciprocity, and the reciprocity of inertia, objectification as it has occurred in different levels of our spiral progress. At the present stage, the true critical question is: what type of existence or being characterizes the concerted action of the organized group, in so far as it is communal, and not in so far as it is resolved into a multiplicity of functions? In brief, what type of intelligibility defines this action? What constitutes its dialectic?

We have seen that the group has no way of acting except in and through the individuals who compose it; and this is possible because group action exists in each individual praxis as interiorized unity of multiplicity. Spatially, each individual praxis as interiorized unity of multiplicity constitutes, that is, brings into being, the ubiquity of the multiplicity of heres. In each single praxis the group action is ubiquitous, everywhere the same, always *here*. Temporally, a similar unification of multiplicity occurs. This entails also a unification of the multiplicity of diachronic temporalizations into a common synthesis, which once more does not exist elsewhere than in each.

As we foreshadowed in the introduction, and as has been the case so far, the comprehension of the dialectic has to be itself a moment of dialectical praxis. So at this point, our individual comprehension of the praxis of organization is itself an exercise in the praxis of the dialectic. Like all other individual praxes, we shall always bear in mind that our act of comprehension is occurring within the group in which we are ourselves situated. The communal means to transcending the seriality and alterity of individual antagonisms and solitudes is constituted as such when the rising external pressure of seriality in each third makes each third, as the necessity of his free action, constitute his praxis as communal, that is, bring into being with each other member of the group who can see the situation as a whole from his perspective, a concerted experience of the field, spatially and temporally, and so realize the conditions of the possibility of free yet co-ordinated group praxis, and in so doing give birth to the group. A fundamental error is to talk as though the group were made up of a number of 'individuals'. This is true only in so far as each individual who constitutes the group does so by a metamorphosis of himself through his interiorization of other interiorizations, the schema for which has already been outlined. The group thus constituted by its own members is a metamorphosis of each individual member who makes it. As a grouped, or communal, individual, all the reciprocal relations of the organized group, the inertia he has taken on himself in the form of functions and powers, rights and obligations, violence-terror and fraternity, are actualized as his new being, as his sociality. His existence is no more a simple temporalization in a project of organic needs. In this sense, the individual is producer of the group, in that the simple organic individual develops into a grouped individual, and at the same time constructs the group through the organization of his field of praxis.

The group as an object can come into view, however, from a position *outside* the group.

Consider the individual hunted by a group. He is pursued and encircled. The organized free praxis of the group is more large, more supple, more powerful, more homogeneous, than his. The field of his praxis is 'mined' by this monstrous freedom. But, whether the group is comprehended by the individual as group-object, group-subject, or practical organism, in every case the common end that the group seems to be pursuing is grasped in practice as that towards which the group transcends the given: and this practical grasp by the individual of the end the group is pursuing is itself *his* transcendence of the group.

Now, we must be careful to note that, as observers of a group from a position as non-members of the group observed, the objective of the group, although common to all its members, appears to us only in and through each group-individual, who is pledged to the group and structured into it. At the same time, *the praxis of each individual who is pledged and structured is not intelligible as a simple singularization of group praxis.*

The pledge, as free limit of freedom, is a token that my own freedom can be turned against me by the others, in so far as it is other for the others. The modality of action of the individual occurring in these terms often eludes the observer outside the group. Loyalty, treachery, fraternity-terror, as lived in another group, we know only from the outside, and we can easily fall into the trap of trying to make praxis, whose intra-group pledged modality is lost to us, intelligible in terms of a non-grouped individual. We must remember that we have to do at this point with the being-in-the-group of an individual metamorphosed by his pledge, that is by his interiorization of the dynamic and inertia of his function within the group. This metamorphosis, as we have said, is not the product of a hyperdialectic. It represents simply a vicissitude in the forms of inter-individual reciprocities.

The pledge is a means of constituting an inertia in the group by utilizing a practical if not theoretical understanding of the structure of reciprocity. In the same way, pledged praxis implies a practical comprehension of the group and of the pledge.[1]

We have not yet found the key to the mystery of the apparent homogeneity of individual and group praxis. How can the group which is so different from a single organic individual produce concerted actions that seem to reflect the same fundamental structure as those of an individual? We see the division and alloca-

---

[1] The father in Sartre's play *Altona* uses his practical comprehension of the reciprocities of the group in order to maintain its inert permanence by the pledge. Almost his first act is to swear the family in on the Bible. He wishes to induce a pledged group even though its individual members do not all realize the violence-terror that they are consenting to, and the metamorphosis that is liable to overtake them.

tion of tasks, regrouping, centralization, and so on. How do they arise? Sometimes they seem to be imposed from above, as it were, sometimes to be forced on the group from below.

The intelligibility of this type of concerted action is the rationality of command-obedience within the context of the whole problem of administration—the 'machinery' for discussion, clarification, classification, planification, the way agreement is reached and 'group' decisions are taken, and the 'machinery' of their implementation.

We must evidently begin to understand dialectically the dialectic of administration. What is the dialectical intelligibility of agreement? Light is thrown on this question if we recall the nature of *group-ubiquity* discussed above. In agreement, the multiplicities of identities disappear, in so far as each comprehension implies all the others. All are realized in each. Ubiquity is a reciprocity of unity. It excludes in one and the same movement the multiple and the identical. *We* agree, not *they* agree. The 'they' are more obviously interchangeable. Each he or she can be the second unity. In saying 'we' this commutativity is a non-explicit content of our unified reciprocity. The group invention of agreement based on the reciprocal unity of 'we' is one form of institutional 'truth' as individual and group operation. Such agreement is impossible under certain circumstances, and techniques of arriving at agreement *between us* can be seen to be quite inappropriate to certain forms of negotiation between *us* and *them*.

There exists in the practical organism a structure of inertia: this permits us to use ourselves as an instrument of our own praxis. But this inertia has nothing in common with the inertia of freedom. The inertia of freedom is the inertia that is itself constituted by freedom and nothing else and *then*, secondarily, becomes the non-dialectical moment of further action.

The ultimate limits of action are prescribed by the nexus of material historical circumstances, not by a pledged inertia which praxis has itself produced. This is crucial.

This inert negation, the inertia that is a product of praxis, represents, however, the *conditio sine qua non* of communal action. It is precisely by it that the group-individual exists. Thus, dialectical praxis as mediation between group-individuals and the work or job to be done, is different from the free solitary praxis of non-grouped organisms, even though they interact reciprocally, to the extent that such individual praxis of grouped individual at once negates, conserves, and actualizes the individual as a power and function in and of the group, that is, the organism as grouped individual.

The group-individual, in actualizing himself as group-individual by his own praxis, is producing himself, forming himself in a field of forces of outrageous violence, which form and deform him far more than he may realize. Yet this 'field of forces' is the group itself in perpetual totalization, never totalized, never a hyper-organism. This 'field of forces' *is* simply the concerted *praxis* of the group. Yet such praxis as a 'force' has certainly lost the trans-lucency of individual praxis. How has this come about? There are no longer any unmediated reciprocities, but reciprocities that have been formed and deformed 'by the group'. Group work has been done on them.

We know the ends which have presided in the pledge: it was a question of struggle against our multiplicity. By interiorizing this multiplicity, by making it submit to unity, concerted action is taken against multiplicity, and we know also that the interioriza-tion of multiplicity is perpetual failure, perpetual redoing and refailure. Right and obligation, in the pledged group, present themselves to dialectical experience and to practical consciousness, as my free alienation of freedom. But this is a statement adequate only for the menace of lapsing into multiplicity, that is being met and reacted to still on the level of the pledge-group, without considering the organized group. We have seen that this menace can be met by a further turn of the spiral, a further self-alienation of my freedom, the invention of a further form of inertia, namely, by the transformation of the pledged group of naked loyalty-treachery, violence-terror-fraternity into permanent organization—if sufficiently permanent, into institutionalization. It is the limits of the intelligibility of this new transformation that we are currently trying to tease out.

Organized praxis is specified by the pyramid of inertias which praxis has itself constituted, and which now seem to constitute it, inside and out. The means of communication in this context are only one example of the separation of interiorities through institutionalized inertia, whether in the form of the exteriorization of the inertia of interiority, or of the interiorization of the inertia of exteriority.

We are now in the midst of industrial complexes considered in the light of human engineering, the group as a machine. The group as a machine is in effect a human product, but the overall operation of the organization of the group is not constitutive dialectical praxis. There are only dialectical and constituting individuals who invent and produce by their work an apparatus, wherein they are enclosed. Concerted organisational praxis is at once a praxis and a process, constituted originally by praxis, but not constitutive of praxis.

Thus we see specific modalities of a group that would be unknown in a solitary person, if such a person could exist—structure, function, power, and, fundamentally, pledge.

Being-in-common can produce in each person new relations with the other, but cannot transform the group itself into an integrating and integral organism. The group remains a multiplicity of practical points of view, which grasp it. In all its forms the group is grasped by these praxes as an inertia. This is the result of the failure in the first moment towards totality. Praxis cannot help but go beyond this inertia, that is, it constitutes itself as the constant *a priori* possibility of the group's dissolution. But we remember that the group *is* the multiplicity of the practical points of view of its members, and this remains true even where, through the interiorization of this multiplicity, this multiplicity is transformed into ubiquity.

Sartre seeks to clarify his position by comparing and contrasting, at this point, praxis and process. He states that they are similar in that:

(i) both are dialectical
(ii) they are defined by their movement and direction
(iii) they transcend the obstacles of the common group field
(iv) both are defined from the starting-point of a certain determination of the field of possibilities which permit the clarification of the signification of their different moments
(v) both are violence, fatigue, perpetual exchange and transmutation of energy.

But, they are dissimilar in that:

(vi) praxis is revealed immediately by its end: the future determination of the field of possibilities is posited from the start by a projective transcendence of material circumstances: i.e. by a project. At each moment of action, it is the agent who produces himself in such or such posture, accompanied by such or such effort in terms of present givens, clarified by his future objective. This praxis is free because in a given circumstance, starting from a given need or danger, it invents its own law, in the absolute unity of its project, as mediation between the objectivity already given, and the objectification that remains to be produced.
(vii) the human group process is neither comparable to an avalanche or an inundation, nor comparable to an individual action. It conserves all the characteristics of individual action, except that of being the free constitution of ends, since it is *constituted by* the orientated action of a multiplicity of individuals. But at the same time, these characteristics receive in it the modification of passivity. Each *here* is presented as a *passivity* in action, and implies the same passivity in a ubiquity in all the *heres*. Praxis appears as the evanescent elsewhere.

Thus there is a leak in the ubiquity of process, a resurrection of multiplicity. For the activity of the other, however much it is evanescent and elsewhere, nevertheless effects a dissolution of the inertia that is being passively undergone *here*, because this activity of the other, in being alterated, is dissolved into the activity of another for whom it is other, and this occurs elsewhere and everywhere; and if the praxis that is needed to dissolve praxis into inertia is itself to be made passive again and once more rendered inert, my own inertia is further dissolved by the activity that I have to undertake in order to produce and maintain this inertia.

In the group, the pledged inertia, as communal praxis, is the always recovered and veiled mediation between organic activities. In the group process practical activity appears as an ungraspable and fleeting event. In all this there is no question of determinism, but a dialectical development intelligible only in terms of the inertia that a multiplicity of agents are inducing in their own concerted actions. To that extent, communal praxis is comprehensible on the same model as individual praxis.

On the other hand, the group process manifests itself as a non-totalized object whose animating movement is not felt by me as emanating from me. Rather, so far as I have my being-beyond-myself-in-the-world, I am subject to it, I undergo it.

Moreover, the process, as something that I undergo, is felt as an objective force which is outside me or which I am outside, that impinges on me. But if one is taken in by this, the process appears not as a synthesis of temporalizations, but as an independent reality in its own right that has become somehow temporalized. That is to say, the process is seen as ruled by a law from outside, and all projective and teleological structures are absorbed into it. But, curiously, this necessity remains orientated, the future remains prefigured, the process conserves its finality, albeit inverted, made passive and masked by necessity. The grasp of group activity as process found in many social theorists rests on a vision of praxis as process. Their group process is an orientated passivity, irreversible, stifled by an inert finality.

The group-process is, from a certain point of view, a constant reality of our experience. The theorists have not invented its characteristics: *they have only chosen to see and study it on the level of its full unintelligibility.*

This unintelligibility is only a moment of intelligibility: it is the initial appearance that certain groups offer. It becomes intelligibility only when it is set in the full context of its dialectic. The process is the inverse of communal praxis. But this represents simply the moment when the interior action of the group on itself is intensified in the struggle against the multiplicity which begins to gnaw at it.

If one considers the process simply in the world, and divorced from the praxis which is its fundamental truth, it reveals aspects new to this investigation, but well-known to the sociologists: schisms and scleroses, useless survivals, local wear and tear, stratifications, homeostasis, group tendencies, conflicts of roles and functions, etc. This side of process marks the limit of its intelligibility. One must enter into this fundamental inertia from the side that faces praxis, and see its opacity, if not as translucid, at any rate as illuminated by intelligibility. The light that intelligibility sheds on process consists in revealing this process-object as the objectified materiality of pledged praxis-subjects. This materiality of the group is something its members are subject to. Yet its members forge it by praxis, and it is forged in and through the very act of subjecting themselves to it in so far as they endure it.

When we consider the relation of praxis to the constituted inertia of the group, it is necessary to remind ourselves that freedom is not the free activity of an autonomous organism, conceived somehow not in any particular situation, but that it is, from its origins, the conquest of alienation. Thus, freedom is sustained, canalized, limited, inside and out, by an inertia both pledged and endured. The absolute limit of organizational praxis is organic and practical individuality, since it is precisely the latter which is constitutive of the former.

There is an ultimate identity, therefore, of individual action and the action of the group, of action of the group and of mechanical action, in that organic praxis is constitutive of group organization, structure and process. And yet, *at the same time*, there is an irreducible opposition between the mechanisms of the group and the individual.

The final problem of intelligibility starts from this: what must a group be in its being such that it appears, by and in itself, to negate individual praxis and ends, and yet such that it can pursue and realize its own communal ends as amplification of the ends freely posited by the practical organisms that have pledged themselves to it, in so far as they are free dialectical existences?

1. *The unity of the group comes from outside by the others, and under this premier form of unity the group exists as an alter*

To the members of a series, a group impinges on them as an erosion of seriality, as an immediate manifestation to which they are subject. A group determines and assumes the appearance of a practical totality at the heart of the external seriality of the non-grouped.

This superficial appearance of the group as totality to those outside it arises also *within* the group, in the midst of alterity (of being other for the other), by the interiorization by each member of the group of the objectivity of the group for the others outside the group. The structure of this incarnation is the inessentiality of the particular individual, and the present essentiality of all in general. We see this in the relation of the militant party member to the Party. This essentially is not lived, however, by the organized member in and for himself. He does not grasp it in the reflexive unity of an organizing act which has, as direct object, the totalization of the group. He produces it by *the mediation of the extra-group others* as the directing schema of his relations with his immediate group other. The party comrade for the militant is not the coessential in a direct reciprocity. The essentiality of all is an empty knowledge, an article of faith, received under sentence

CRITIQUE OF DIALECTICAL REASON

of imposed inertia, interiorized in abstract oath, and re-exteriorized in stereotyped actions, or in relational structures tending toward stereotypy. The militant tries to relate, as accident to substance, every particular circumstance to the Party as a substantial totality. The Party is a crucible for dissolving into the inessential every particular concrete reality.

The praxis, then, of the militant is constituted by the mediation of the out-group other between the in-group individual and the group-as-object-for-the-out-group-other interiorized by the in-group subject, and the mediation of this interiorized group-object between the in-group individual as agent and the out-group other as object of his action.

2. *In the interiority of the group, the movement of mediated reciprocity constitutes the unity of the practical community as a perpetual detotalization engendered by the totalizing movement*

The false bond of interiority, whereby the group constitutes for each an anti-subjective substance whose being is defined at one and the same time by inertia and by obligation to it, has to be contrasted to the true bond of interiority of reciprocity, albeit that this too is necessarily a mediated one.

In the interiority of the being-of-the-group, a new statute of intelligibility comes into view through *the third inside the group*, in contrast to *the third as other outside the group*, whose interiorization of the group-object and the reinteriorization of this interiorization by each member of the group gives the group the appearance of the objective totality just described.

In the pledge, considered dyadically, each undertakes to remain the same, but inescapably the unity of such duality is detotalized by the two totalizing centres themselves. Now let us amplify this account in terms of the third.

Consider A and B in a common action, totalizing themselves reciprocally with the group and in the group, by a reciprocity mediated in and through the group. The in-group third is ex-

cluded from the dyad, but is also regulative of it. For each person
in the dyad interiorizes the dyad as a quasi-objective totality,
through interiorizing the interiorization of the dyad as object for
the third. But the third is in turn a member of a dyad, and A and
B of the first dyad totalize the dyad that C now makes with D, and
so on. Thus, there is inclusion and exclusion, totalization, detotalization, retotalization, interiorization, interiorization of interiorization, and interiorization of interiorization of interiorization. *The
third* can be me, you, or him: me as other, he as me, you as him,
the interiorization by me of him and her. Her interiorization of
him and me: his interiorization of her interiorization of him
and me—all this is merely a slight indication of the infinite compression that the interiorized other-for-the-other undergoes in
the interiority of the group.

Being-in-the-group, in its interiority, is manifested by a double
failure to which each has given his consent: powerlessness to leave,
and powerlessness to be integrated: powerlessness to dissolve the
group in oneself, or to be dissolved in it. And *this double failure is
the very basis of practical unity, which is the absolute contradiction of
ontological unity.*

Yet the oneness of the group exists, in so far as the inertia to
which each person has committed himself is the same in each.
This inert being is seen to be a serrated line of inert mediated
reciprocities, in that my own freedom becomes other by the
mediation of the other, and is a means of producing practical
differentiation. This apparent inertia, however, is fundamentally
a practical organization, and exists only by praxis. This organization, to be intelligible, must be grasped as practical differentiation.
But it can also be viewed with the praxis that generates it bracketed
off; then the group turns into a collection of inert-means, and its
practical organization is transformed into a skeletal structure of
relations treatable by an ordinal calculus, and group events are
seen only as processes. The possibility of this illusion, moreover, is
given in the essential structure of all communities.

The profound contradiction at all levels is that real unity is

CRITIQUE OF DIALECTICAL REASON

concerted *praxis, not* this reduction to inertia. As we have seen above, practical unity is an absolute contradiction of ontological unity. A second reason for the illusion of the unity of the group as an inert totality has also been adumbrated, namely, that the group, for the non-grouped, and for other groups, appears as a living objective totality, and the interiorization by the group of its being-for-the-other and even of its being-for-other-for-other[1] leads to a semblance of totalized unity which is really the infinite compression of the interiorized group as other-for-the-others, whereby the group, as it were, tries to make itself a totalized unity for itself. In so doing, however, it merely makes itself, as interiorized other for the collective others, the object of its own ignorance.

The pledge, my commitment to the group of my own future, is the mother of all institutions, but what transformations have to occur before the organization becomes an hierarchical institution? Now, the basis of terror is that the group cannot have the unitary ontological statute that it claims for itself in its praxis. This non-existent totality is a sort of empty interior. It is the incurable malaise, as it were, of all groups. For instance, as a pledged member of an organized group I fulfil a function, say, I execute a foreign mission on its behalf. The praxis that has to fulfil the mission immediately gives me the possibility of treachery or the fear of the imputation of treachery and possible exile. But in the interior of the group, the regulative and regulated action of each as third,

---

[1] Sartre appears to be dealing with what I have called a meta-meta-meta-perspective, or even fourth-level perspectives:

p = in-group person
o = out-group person
G = group

either:

$p \longrightarrow G$	$o \longrightarrow G$
p's view of group	o's view of group
$p \longrightarrow (o \longrightarrow G)$	$o \longrightarrow (p \longrightarrow (o \longrightarrow G))$
p's view of o's view of group	o's view of p's view of o's view of group

$p \longrightarrow (o \longrightarrow (p \longrightarrow (o \longrightarrow G)))$
p's view of o's view of p's view of o's view of G

or:

$p \longrightarrow G$	$o \longrightarrow (p \longrightarrow G)$
$p \longrightarrow (o \longrightarrow (p \longrightarrow G)$	$o \longrightarrow (p \longrightarrow (o \longrightarrow (p \longrightarrow G)))$

$p \longrightarrow (o \longrightarrow (p \longrightarrow (o \longrightarrow (p \longrightarrow G))))$ (see Laing, 1961, op. cit.).

the integration by each third and integration of each third, sets up a revolving exclusion, a circular succession of exiles for all and for each within the group itself, even without formal coalitions of alliances. I realize in my relations with the thirds my tension of immanence-transcendence as truth of our human relations, and this truth is that I cannot truly ever be completely *in* the group, or, at least, that my being-in is not to be grasped under the naive form of content to a container. My being-in-the-group is that of an excluded-included, regulating-regulated third, and this is my exile in the very interior of the group I am most inside. The regulative act of each third is simultaneously an intercession and a secession. My separation as third from the others is endured as a sort of inertia, and this reinforces the pledged inertia to which I have sworn myself.

Free individuality is the unique means towards, and the unique obstacle to, the constitution of the organized group. We shall see presently that it is only in and through praxis that a further statute of inertia appears in the group, when the organized group starts its self-transformation into an institution. This is the resurrection of seriality once more in the heart of unity, on a new level. Organization becomes institution, organized individual becomes institutionalized individual, the mediated reciprocities of the organized group becomes serial links of thirds who are all in exile. And this intensification of the inorganic inside the group is precisely its struggle against the inorganic, against dissolution, dispersion, death.

It is on this level that the institution is defined, or, to preserve our conducting thread, that certain practical necessities in the organized group are given a new ontological statute in being institutionalized.

In the living moment of the group, the group individual is not inessential, since he is the same in all, that is, the dispersed multiplicity of the group is negated by the praxis of unity. Each is then the bearer of the same essentiality. But in the degraded group, each is constituted as inessential in relation to his function.

The group undergoes two basic transformations in the transition from organization to institution:

1. The transformation of the mediated reciprocities outlined in respect of the pledged organized group into a new form of institutional seriality.
2. As the organization is transformed into a sovereign institution, the power that is lost to the individual in his subordination to this new form of serial impotence is lodged in an institutional locus of power.

This latter transformation raises the problem of the intelligibility of the institutionalized hierarchical power system.

The institution, as rebirth of seriality and impotence, must consecrate power to assure its permanence by law. Its authority rests on inertia and seriality. The institutionalized power hierarchy is neither a praxis, nor a process. The *institution* is an inorganic unification of a serialized multiplicity. The *sovereign* is the dissolution, and synthetic reunification of exterior inorganic passivity in the organic unity of his regulative praxis. His authority is the individual reincarnation, on this new level, of the group-infusion and of freedom-terror.

The contradiction of the sovereign is that he both sustains the institution by his praxis, and that this praxis is itself a product of the inert eternity of institutional relations.

One can fall into the trap of starting from the state of massification where the absence of relation has become the fundamental relation, and to generalize from there without seeing this massification in its dialectical intelligibility.

The sole limitation of the lordship of one man over the others is simple reciprocity, namely, the entire lordship of each over each. This original relation, when it is lived outside any institution, comes back to constituting every man as absolute over any other man whatsoever. This reciprocity is a co-sovereignty. The concentration of power in institutionalized sovereignty negates direct reciprocity through the centralization of power, and is a further alienation of the already indirect mediated reciprocity of the organization.

Yet organic praxis remains, in spite of all the masks, the sole ultimate modality of action. When I obey an order, my freedom destroys itself freely and strips itself of its translucency to actualize here, in my muscles, in my body at work, the freedom of the other. It is the freedom of the *other*, whether elsewhere, in the other, or lived here by me, that is signified by my action. It is the inflexible absence and absolute priority, everywhere, of interiorized alterity—everywhere except, of course, in this final Other, who is other than all to the precise extent that he alone has power to be himself.

Thus, the institution, as the reifying mediation between men who have become passive, sets up the institution of a man as mediation between its own institutions. The sovereign is the reflexive synthesis of dead praxes. Through unconditioned fidelity, respect, fear, adoration, there is concentrated in him alone allegiance-terror as struggle against seriality. The sovereign does not impose his power on an organized group but on an impotent series. He exploits the inertia of relations. *His power is not based on acceptance, but the acceptance of his power is the interiorization of the powerlessness to refuse it.* A new form of alienation comes into view through this petrified series of institutionalized men when the institutional group comes in contact with the diverse serialities of the non-grouped. The incarnation of sovereignty by the group occurs when the end pursued by the sovereign is truly the common object of the group. In this new moment of experience the efficacy of the group's action on the impotence and dispersion of its objects (the extra-group serialities) is mediated through the sovereign in so far as the objective end of the group has been incarnated in his ends, so that he and the institution are One. I am the State.

The mystifications at the heart of this diffused sovereignty are in forgetting that serial impotence is the necessity of freedom, and in believing that by incarnating the State in the sovereign, or sovereignty in the State, something more than a phantom unity of a congealed serialized mass is achieved.

Real individual praxis is always suspect to any member of the serialized mass, and in terms of institutional mystification it must be destroyed. Praxis remains, however, as transcendent freedom. The fundamental nature of institutionalization, its serial impotence, separation and reification, sovereign and serialized mass, in fact reveal, through the lucidity of their intelligibility, once de-mystified, a further form of alienation of our individual freedom.

3. *Dialectical experience as totalization: the level of the concrete, the place of history*

The group is produced through the more or less profound dissolution of discrete multiplicity in the unity of concerted praxis. The object of this praxis can be defined only in terms of (i) other groups, mediated or not by series, (ii) inorganic circumstances, mediated or not by other groups, and (iii) worked matter (*matière ouvrée*), mediated or not by series and by groups.

The praxis of the group outside itself, its objectification of itself, reveals three principal characteristics.

1. New and unifying practical realities in the social and physical materiality constituting its practical field are *created* as soon as the group acts outside itself. Changes in other groups can be direct or indirect. Since the field of the group's action is a synthetic unity of practical totalization, and is such for each group, the apparition, even at a distance, of another group as non-totalizable retotalizations of its own field, is a permanent menace of radical *alteration* of all the interior references in its own system. This gives the basis for indirect change, which is liable to occur without any direct action of one group on the other.

2. Through this *group alteration*, the group's synthetic achievements are necessarily alienated. The Army is victorious, and yet the mere presence of the conquered gives the field of battle a

polyvalence which strips the object of all univocal and uncontested signification. Any object produced by the group in any sense is itself multidimensional. The common field is a multidimensional occasion of insecurity. This mediation between the objective field and the group does not lead to historical scepticism, but it does mean that the integration of these multiple significations can be achieved only in a perspective which will permit the integration of all the groups, that is, in a historical perspective.

The multiplicity of groups gives us a plurality of temporalizations. The dialectic of different temporalizations gives us the concept of *diachronicity*. The aftermath of the 1914-1918 war in France and Germany reveals a step-by-step synchronous alienation of its results in both countries, when the new generation in both countries construed victory or defeat differently from their fathers, and these totalizations were equally alien to each other.

3. The group stamps the outside with the inertia it wishes to suppress in itself, and in so doing actualizes this inertia within itself. The client, as serial object, must be manipulated, but in order to manipulate the client, the salesman manipulates himself. Seriality, then, can be envisaged in two dimensions. Vertical: hierarchical group, manipulations of manipulations; and horizontal: external seriality of manipulanda.

When the man-of-the-group acts on the men-outside-the-group as a serial mass, the moment of his total objectivity as man-for-himself altered to other-for-other is not reinteriorized as pure transcended condition of dialectical action. He is congealed in his stance and his manipulation of the other precludes him from full awareness of how the other perceives him.

We are now at the threshold of achieving dialectical experience and a schema adequate to the intelligibility of the historical concrete, but at present we have before us still only the formal and the abstract. The individual as abstract reality finds his first more concrete characteristics in alienation in the practico-inert, and this materiality, this non-dialectical density of being, has given him the occasion to invent sociality. This sociality is the work done by men on men, by groups on groups and series. It becomes the violence of emerging alienated freedom, and violence on this violence.

The study of different structures, in order of increasing complexity, has shown us the continued re-emergence of inertia in the group, first as free violence of freedoms against themselves in order to find themselves a common being in a reciprocally forged inertia. This is what Sartre has called freedom as necessity. From this point, this necessity, produced by freedom itself, freely consented to, under pressure of circumstances of increasing urgency, and under the shadow of scarcity, becomes, as it were, the very driving force in a spiral of inertia. Necessity is made into the agent of the exteriorization of the interiorized inertia of the pledged group by the creation of institutionalized relations, until the statute proper to institutionalization in turn produces the conditions and means of a further re-interiorization. The sequence of dialectical experience has shown us that sovereignty as agent of petrification is the consequence of, and the essential factor in, an increase in seriality, but that this seriality is not simply the formal development of pledged inertia in material conditions which require it. The group, as a multiplicity of reciprocities upon which work has been done, is a product of men, not a given of nature, but the necessity of freedom implies a progressive alienation of freedom to necessity.

Collectives are not found in experience as we left them in abstracted form. The series, concretely, has always been further worked upon by recurrent mystifications, and is massified into a sort of mystified synthesis of quasi-inorganic materiality. It bears the brand or imprint of the practical unity of the petrified group that has worked it over.

But the group, to grasp it in its profound origin, is produced in the project of stripping worked-matter of its inhuman power of mediation between men, to return it in community to each and to all, and in the attempt to grasp the practical field (things and collectives) by free concerted praxis.

The project of forming a group in concrete circumstances will entail the erosion of mystified and massified seriality. It will be the project of snatching man from the statute of alterity, which makes of him a product of his product, to transform him into his own producer and product.

Need and scarcity, under the shadow of serial impotence, are the negative possibility of the group. *The group is a possible mode of existence*, as an instrument and as a free context for free human relations. Starting from the pledge, men produce the group by producing themselves as men-of-the-group. At that moment the group confers on the other his new birth. Thus, the group is at once the most effective instrument for mastering the material field under the shadow of scarcity, and as concerted pure freedom for liberating men from alterity.

There is thus a fundamental reciprocity between the group and the series in the interiorizing of the group in the series, and the interiorizing of the series in the group. Both sides of this reciprocity are the basic problem of the revolutionary party. There is something of osmosis in this dialectical transmutation. The series infects the group with its passivity, which the group interiorizes and either transforms it into an instrument for its own survival, or is destroyed by it.

We have already touched on some of the strange appearances that can arise in the course of this dialectic—those mirages of totality, pseudo-syntheses, phantom unities, and those pseudo-unities of exterior series e.g. the consumers. This dialectic of groups and series is, as we have seen, constituted in turn by praxis. This has a double circularity.

(1) The first circularity is static. The structure and lines of action of the group are defined by the characteristics of the series from which it has been plucked. Alterity and passive activity are used as instruments of action. The rhythm of production (like the movement of the machines) is an instrument of production.

(2) The second circularity is the perpetual movement which degrades sooner or later the groups-in-action, and makes them fall into seriality.

This latter circularity is without any pre-given law whatsoever. It has no necessary sequence. A group-in-fusion may dissolve into seriality immediately, or go on through a pledged group to become an institution. Just as possibly, the institution may arise directly from a serial collective. It is this double circularity, static and dynamic, in so far as it is manifested in the revolving relations at all levels of all social concretions, that institutes the terminal moment of dialectical experience, and, by the same token, the concrete reality of sociality.

This concrete moment of experience reintegrates all the abstract moments which we have reached and transcended one after the other: it puts them back at the heart of the concrete in their concrete function. First, the free praxis of the isolated individual loses its suspect character of Robinson Crusoe: *there is no* pure, single individual. Solitude is a peculiar structure of sociality. In historical totalization, the real disappearance of the isolated individual on behalf of the Other, or of the communal individual, or of a function, is made on the basis of organic praxis as constituting dialectic. We will *never meet* the isolated individual except implicitly and negatively as a relative moment of the constituted dialectic, that is, as the fundamental absence of any ontological guarantee of group oneness, as evidenced, for instance, by the exile of a man of the group, or in the paradoxical aim to dissolve the multiplicity of persons in the cult of personality.

If the isolated individual is an abstraction, the collectives so far studied are no less abstract. The pastorals of certain anthropologists about Society are on a par with the Robinson Crusoe type of myth that is such anathema to them. They do not realize that the 'Society' of their discourse is as abstracted and as extrapolated as the 'individual' considered out of context, that is, not in his concrete reality. The group without series and series without group are both abstractions. The circularity of the conversions between series and group precludes, as we stated above, any *a priori* law of sequence. But there is an *a priori* necessity that there should be a perpetual double movement of regroupment and petrification. Sartre's basic question, however, has not been what empirically actually does or does not take place, or has or has not taken place in a particular historical concrete circumstance, but the intelligibility of what could, can, may, possibly occur.

At this stage, then, we can ask whether among the social realities that we have studied so far there is a specific statute for certain realities whose real unity will manifest itself as a link of interiority between group multiplicities and serial multiplicities. We remember that seriality wedded to inorganic matter defines a field we have called the practico-inert. The historical production of groups brings into being new forms of social fields. The action of group on series, for instance, produces 'the mass'. Now, the possibility of social class is a new type of social reality given by the interpenetration of various multiplicities. Have they all already been described?

The being-of-class (the working class of nineteenth-century French capitalism is Sartre's main example) is defined by the seriality of impotence, in so far as it is qualified and determined by practico-inert exigencies. The original and negative relation of worker to the machine—its non-possession by him, the mystification of free contract, the fact that work becomes an enemy force for the worker, his serial dispersion and the antagonistic reciprocities on the labour-market, all this characterizes a situation reminiscent of seriality and the practico-inert.

However, this serial statute of the practico-inert could not produce a class struggle if the permanent possibility of dissolving the series were not given to each. A first and abstract determination of this possible unity was given by class interest, as negative possibility of destiny, as when we say: 'None of us wants this to happen to us.'

However, the transformation of a class into a pure group without any admixture of seriality at any level, is never realized, even in a revolutionary period. The syndical group is typical of the organized group that becomes institutional and sovereign. Even anarcho-syndicalism demands a workers' élite. The working class at moments of its greatest possible 'solidarity' involves groups-in-fusion, pledged groups of reciprocal loyalty, and inert seriality, in certain sectors profoundly penetrated by the haunted unity of pledged groupings, institutionalized organization, and even institutions.

Now, our consideration of our abstract possibilities is, of course, being conducted so that we can pose better the question of the intelligibility of the concrete. Is there a difficulty in posing the intelligibility of the class considered concretely? Is it too complicated to be intelligible? Let us look at this carefully. A social class is manifested simultaneously under three statutes:

  (i) institutionalized apparatus

 (ii) groups (partly still serial, partly organized) of groups-in-fusion and pledged groups

(iii) a series stamped in and through the relations of production with the statute of the practico-inert field by other classes.

These three statutes unified in a universal schema give us the triple reality of the historical nineteenth-century working class in movement. But in this meeting of the group as dialectic constituted by praxis, and of series as anti-dialectic to praxis and group, do we reach the very limits of intelligibility, and even if the formal intelligibility of these dialectical determinations is admitted, is it possible to grasp the reciprocal transformations of its practical modalities, or is the complication too great?

Sartre states that if we examine the conditions of the possibility of individual comprehension, we shall see that the answer is no. The first necessity for the investigator (in supposing that he has the necessary information, etc.) is that he comprehend the comprehension of the regulative third. He must:

  (i) have a grasp of the free praxis of the group—a transcendence that conserves the conditions of the transcended;

(ii) understand the project of the other group in its unity for itself;

(iii) grasp, in a new comprehension, the conditions transcended as determination at the heart of the group. That is, the conditions once transcended are seen in the completely new light of the project that has transcended these conditions.

The unique limit of the power of comprehension is set here not by the complexity of the object, but by the situation of the observer. This signifies that comprehension defines a double objectivity: its own and that of the group which is its object. But this limit of principle and of fact is in no way a factor of less intelligibility. On the contrary, if the dialectic of the project of understanding another project is not to founder in dogmatism it must be produced as practical relation between free organisms in a situation. It is as organism positioned in a situation that I comprehend, across my own situation as conditioning my own project, the comprehension of the other, and his dependence on his own location within his own situation.

When the praxis of the pledged group is the concerted expression of each person's avowed intention, we can grasp the dialectic of a multiplicity of projects, often in antagonistic interaction, each refracting partial significations in the inside of the concurrent group totalization. The pledged group is riddled with the revolving oppositions of the regulator-third at the heart of every reciprocity within the group.

The command-obedience-unity structure of institutional groups is an attempt to resolve this, and praxis-in-fusion is the perpetual reinvention of the group in and through the thirds. The only difference in the comprehension of an end achieved by praxis and a process that defeats the achievement of an end is that the latter has no author. But does this absence of author rob the authorless praxis of signification? Is this a mere epiphenomenon, an anthropomorphic illusion? Process deprived of meaning is often taken to be the positive truth of so-called human action. But the positive viewpoint of analytic reason is the negative limit of the constituted dialectic.

Now, in the above, Sartre has examined praxis in greatest detail on the level of the pledged group, and this has been examined only partially. Praxis, considered more concretely in terms of class, entails, as we saw, different levels, for a class is praxis and inertia, dispersion of alterity, common field for another class.

What are the practical possibilities within a series of the resurrection of praxis, when each practical organism, always ungraspable and hidden by alienation and seriality, is whirling in circuits of alterity?

A new type of praxis has to be envisaged, a praxis whose unitary and dialectic temporalization, starting from the objective to be attained, is developed in the unity of multi-dimensional reciprocities between heterogenous structures, of which each contains the others in itself. Or, if one wishes an image, the action of the free practical organism is temporalized in a space of n dimensions.

Praxis remains constitutive, but with the necessary contradiction that the number of its dimensions enters into conflict with the non-transcendability of free organic praxis as the generator of the constituting dialectic.

The process—on this level—is the undetermined being of totalization grasped from the outside, which can be neither pure dialectical development of a free praxis, nor totalized totality, nor irreversible and non-signifying series of determinations in exteriority, but that which by reason of this same indetermination, presents itself as the abstract possibility of a union of all these characters.

It would be absurd to substantiate the process, this fusion of sense and nonsense, to give a positive content to this abstract limit of comprehension, and to suppress the contradictions of experience in considering man from the point of view of God.

The process is rigorously bound to the situation by the agent. The situation defines it negatively by its limits, and there can be no question of grasping it by desituating ourselves in relation to everything. There is no way to integrate the project of a social multiplicity except by an individualizing schema.

B. CONCLUSIONS: THE INDIVIDUAL IN A CLASS SOCIETY

A man is a practical organism living with a multiplicity of similar organisms in a field of scarcity. But this scarcity is a negative force that defines each man and each partial multiplicity as human and inhuman realities at one and the same time.

Each individual, for example, in so far as he risks consuming a product of first necessity for me (and for all the others) risks becoming one-too-many. He threatens my life to the extent that he is my double: he becomes then inhuman in so far as he is man. My species becomes an alien species.

Through reciprocity and interchangeability I discover in the field of my possibilities the possibility of being myself objectively made by the others into one-too-many, or as an inhuman form of the human. The praxis of the other, comprehensible and threatening, is what I must destroy in him. But this praxis, as dialectical organization of the means to satisfy need, is manifested as free development of action in the other, and we know that it is this freedom, as my freedom in the other, that we must destroy to avoid the risk of death, which is the original bond between men by mediation of matter. Otherwise said, the interiorization of scarcity as mortal relation of man to man is itself achieved by a free dialectical transcendence of material conditions, and in this very transcendence freedom manifests itself as the practical organization of the field and as the freedom of the other that is to be destroyed as anti-praxis and anti-value.

Violence is the action of freedom on freedom by the mediation of inorganic matter. Free praxis can directly destroy the freedom of the other, or put it in parenthesis, as it were, by mystifications and stratagems. Violence can also be action against the necessity of alienation, or be exercised against one's own or the other's freedom, in order to forestall the possibility of falling into seriality. Violence, whether against contra-man, against one's brother, as freedom to annihilate freedom, as terror-fraternity, etc. in every case is a reciprocal recognition of freedom and negation (reciprocal or univocal) of freedom by the intermediary of the inertia of exteriority.

On the level of the class struggle we have to do with oppression and exploitation, and in all such activities, Sartre has abstracted three modalities of human action—individual, group, and praxis-process—so that it is possible to envisage the same developments as e.g. oppression and exploitation as praxis and process. There is need also to take the precaution of defining the modes of rationality that one utilizes in dissolving analytic reason in the constituted dialectic, or in grasping the circularity of the transformations and vicissitudes of praxis and showing its alienation at all levels, as a series of necessities of which it is at once the mystified victim and the fundamental ground.

It is possible to conceive, logically and formally, a universe where practical multiplicities are not constituted into classes. But if they exist, then it is necessary to choose to define them either in inert terms as strata of society and without unity other than the inert compactness of geological corpses: or, as moving, changing, receding, ungraspable, and yet real, units, deriving from positive and negative practical reciprocity with other classes. Sartre chooses the hypothesis of two classes in the negative reciprocity of conflict.

The unity of the class is the circularity of a movement of mediation, such that seriality itself, despite its receding alterity, becomes the mediating link between institutional and pledged groups.

Recently, the possessing class has found a new stratagem of mystification (falsification and alteration of freedom) by way of neo-paternalism, and human engineering. In the face of the intellectual idealism of the analytic reason of the bourgeoisie, the worker must re-invent reason to oppose to a bourgeois-intellectual criterion of truth. The petit bourgeois intellectual and the prole-tarian intellectual are both, of course, liable to perpetuate various mystifications of their own. On a certain level of abstraction, the conflict of classes expresses itself in a conflict of rationalities.

Science, so far, has been a bourgeois venture. There is nothing particularly dialectical about its form of reason, and it does not seem to be in need of it either. But it is quite another thing when it is the human scene itself that is in question. Here, the dialectic is grasped by the practical consciousness of the oppressed class of its struggle. It *has* to be the transcendence of a contemplative truth by a practical and efficacious one, the transcendence of atomizing and massifying truth (e.g. serial concurrence) by the synthetic unity of the combat group.

This practical comprehension by the worker is the 'objective mentality' of the working class in so far as it is invented as extreme urgency and necessary negation of sub-humanity. The intel-lectuals who tell them this are the traitors of the oppressing class. The only intelligibility of human relations is dialectical: and this dialectic, in a concrete history whose truth is based on scarcity, must manifest itself in an antagonistic reciprocity between classes.

A struggle, on the individual level, was seen as a two-headed temporalization of reciprocity. Is there not, strictly, a sort of intimate negation at the heart of this monster, each thwarting and mystifying the other, each seeking to disarm the freedom of the other, and to make him into one's unconscious accomplice, each recognizing the sovereignty of the other only to have the chance of treating him like a thing?

If it is possible to decipher this antagonistic reciprocity in individuals, can this be done with the praxis-process of classes? As soon as praxis loses its awareness of end and means, and this entails the ends and means of its adversary, and the means of opposing this adverse praxis—it becomes blind, ceases to be praxis but becomes the unconscious accomplice of other action which overflows it, manipulates it, alienates it, and turns it round against its own agent as enemy force.

In a sense, the fundamental intelligibility of the struggle represents a development of dialectical comprehension: it implies necessarily that the praxis of each adversary is determined as a function of its own objectivity for the other—in the atomized, massified, or serialized crowds which enclose us, our reality as subject remains abstract, since our practical impotence paralyzes us, and our reality as object resides in the other.

The subject-object relation generates variable tension, and although it is not necessarily expressed in discourse, it is immediately given in reciprocally antagonistic praxis. I comprehend the enemy starting from the object I am for him, that is, from my grasp of my position as object-for-him, and of the other as subject.

A struggle implies reciprocal recognition by each of the following: the recognition of the action of the other starting from the inorganic reality of the conditions where the other is found: the recognition of one's own action against the other, starting from one's inert and material conditions that are one's point of departure; each person must comprehend the other's comprehension.

The struggle is the only human practice that realized *urgently* the relation of each to his being-as-object. That is, the dialectical intelligibility of a project comprehends in it the comprehension of the project of the other. There are two free projects—two transcendencies of transcendence. Man is the being by whom man is reduced to the state of a hated object. The transformation of the other into a non-human object—man and the destruction of man —are given as reciprocal abstracts.

The praxis of the struggle is thus given in each person's case as his comprehension of his being-as-an-object. The struggle as a reciprocity is a function of the reciprocity of comprehensions. If one of the adversaries ceases to comprehend, he becomes simply a manipulable object of the other. In the struggle, each person is a negation of negation, aiming not only to transcend his own being as an object, but to liquidate the other for whom he is an object, and thus recoup his objectivity. Thus, antagonistic negation is grasped in each as a sort of scandal. There is a scandal in the recognition that the other negates my negation of his negation—in the recognition that he recognizes me by his perpetual detotalization of my totalization of him.

The scandal is not in the simple existence of the other, but in the violence undergone or threatened in each person's perception of the other as one-too-many through interiorized scarcity. Under the rubric of interiorized scarcity the rationality of the praxis of each is the rationality of violence. Here, violence is not a simple, naïve ferocity of man, but the comprehensible reinteriorization of each of the contingent fact of scarcity.

Finally, what is the rationality of the comprehension by a *third* of the struggle? Can he realize by his mediation a transcendent and objective unity of positive reciprocities? Here we come to the beginning of our next task, history as such. For history is the totalization of all the practical multiplicities and of their struggles, and the extent of its intelligibility is the dialectical limit of the praxis-process of the different practical structures and the different forms of active multiplicities that between them lie.

But that is a story that we can only now perhaps begin to tell.

totalization, 9 ff., 101
  how constituted, 13, 27
  dialectical reason as, 102
  by different individuals, 108 ff.
  and history, 93, 103 ff.
  Lewin and, 47
  mediated by matter, 112
  and totality, 103
tourniquets, 86, 87
treachery, 82
treason, 135, 137
truth, as becoming, 39

ubiquity,
  group-, 150
  unity as, 132
unification, unifying and unified, 102
unintelligibility, of group-process,
  155

unity, practical and ontological, 158 f.
universals, singularized, 103
U.S.S.R., 37

Valéry, Paul, 43 f.
value categories, opposed, 76 f.
vampirism, magical, 81
Vico, G., 12
violence, 114, 133, 136, 165, 172 f.,
  176

Whitehead, A. N., 96
Wittgenstein, L., 17
worker, and machine, 168
World War I, aftermath of, 164

Znaniecki, F., 22

R. D. LAING is the author of *The Politics of Experience, The Divided Self, Knots, Facts of Life,* and many other books. After studying medicine at Glasgow University, he practiced as a psychiatrist in the British army and as a physician at the Glasgow Royal Mental Hospital, and taught at the University of Glasgow. Subsequently, he joined the Tavistock Clinic and was later appointed director of the Langham Clinic in London. From 1961 to 1967 he undertook research into families, and he is now in private practice as a psychoanalyst.

D. G. COOPER was born in Cape Town, South Africa, and educated at the University of Cape Town, where he earned his degrees in medicine and chemistry. A founder with R. D. Laing of the Philadelphia Association, he was also a director of the Institute of Phenomenological Studies and a practicing psychotherapist in London. The author of *The Death of the Family* and *Psychiatry and Anti-Psychiatry,* he is now a professor at the University of Paris at Vincennes.

Books by Simone de Beauvoir Forthcoming in Pantheon Paperback

WHEN THINGS OF THE SPIRIT COME FIRST
Five Early Tales
translated by Patrick O'Brien

The first paperback edition of the marvelous early fiction of Simone de Beauvoir. These five short stories illuminate the climate in which De Beauvoir grew up, the origins of her thought, and the fascinating young mind of the woman who was to become one of the cultural giants of her day.

"An event for celebration." —*The New York Times Book Review*

"Tales told with remarkably clear-eyed moral vision and pungent irony: a worthy opening to a shining career." —*Kirkus Reviews*
0-394-72235-3

THE WOMAN DESTROYED
translated by Patrick O'Brien

Three stories on the theme of woman's vulnerability: to the process of aging; to loneliness; and to the growing indifference of a loved one. A compelling and disturbing reflection of De Beauvoir's understanding of older women.

"Witty, immensely adroit....These three women are believable individuals presented with a wry mixture of sympathy and exasperation." —*The Atlantic*

"Immensely intelligent stories about the decay of passion."
—*The London Sunday Times*
0-394-71103-3

Forthcoming in Hardcover

ADIEUX
translated by Patrick O'Brien

Simone de Beauvoir's farewell to Jean-Paul Sartre. Part I is an extraordinarily moving account of the last ten years of his life—his relationship with her, his political and intellectual work, his friends, his death. Part II is De Beauvoir's interview with Sartre—one of the most candid he has ever given—conducted a few years before his death. With astonishing perspective, he reviews his life and his thoughts on love, politics, women, philosophy, and literature.

0-394-53035-7